SUCCESS

...AS A SECOND LANGUAGE

A Guidebook for Defining and Achieving Personal Success

Valerie Alexander

Valerie Alexander (signature)

This book is also available as an eBook.
Visit www.SpeakHappiness.com for details.

Author Photo by Samantha Ronceros
Cover Design by Valerie Alexander
Cover Layout by Joshua Barragan
Interior Layout by Ramesh Kumar Pitchai

ISBN-13: 978-1503178076
ISBN-10: 1503178072

TABLE OF CONTENTS

PREFACE

WHAT MAKES SOMEONE A SUCCESS?

What would be the point of reading a book about success from a person who is not successful? That's like reading a cookbook by someone who's never prepared food.

I find it both amusing and ironic that so many of the books, articles, blogs, webinars and workshops offered today along the lines of "Ten Steps to Instant Success" are by people whose only success comes from selling the "secrets" to success. Good for them! They're probably doing what they love, and making money at it, so I guess that's proof that they know how to be successful, themselves. But what can they teach *you*?

Some will swear you have to get up earlier every day, some say get more sleep, then a new study comes out claiming that the most accomplished people are night owls. One article demands that you "ruthlessly block out distractions," while another touts multi-tasking at all times as the way to get ahead. Should you have a laser-like focus on a single goal? What is the ideal number of phone calls or the right amount of time spent networking to ensure your prosperity? Is prosperity the true measure of success? Is success even attainable or is it an ever-moving goal line?

Here's the absolute truth: No one knows!

Every path to success looks different, and every definition of success is unique. That's what this book is about. It's about YOU, and how you define success, and how you can get there, and how to recognize it once you arrive. All of the tips, techniques and exercises in these pages are designed to get you closer to your own success.

The external metrics that society uses to designate who is top dog and who isn't have nothing to do with your journey, your goals and your achievements. Is the CEO who chose not to get married so that she could travel more and work longer hours a success? What about the person who quit his mid-level management job to stay at home with his children? How would you rate the one who gave up a six-figure income to paint for a living and now lives in an industrial loft instead of a 4,000 square-foot mansion? Who among these people is a success? All of them? None?

In the past 18 years, I have been a securities lawyer, a consultant, an investment banker, my mother's caretaker, a screenwriter, a film director, an author, speaker and life coach. In every one of those jobs, you could say I've been successful, or you could say I've failed. It all depends on your point of view. So I'll share my journey with you in Chapter One, and let you decide for yourself.

Where I have truly succeeded along the way is in spotting the moments that matter while still in them, paying attention to the lessons of those moments, and remembering and distilling them enough to help others on their paths. Those lessons are the core of this book. In the next pages, you will learn how I got to where I am today, what I knew that got me there, and what I didn't know (and often didn't know I didn't know) that was holding me back. All of it is designed to be applicable to your life, your journey, and your own quest to define and achieve success.

DON'T QUIT

by Edgar A. Guest

When things go wrong, as they sometimes will,
When the road you're trudging seems all uphill,
When the funds are low and the debts are high,
And you want to smile but you have to sigh,
When care is pressing you down a bit –
Rest if you must,
But don't you quit.

Life is queer with its twists and turns.
As everyone of us sometimes learns.
And many a fellow turns about
When he might have won had he stuck it out.

Don't give up though the pace seems slow –
You may succeed with another blow.
Often the goal is nearer than
It seems to a faint and faltering man;

Often the struggler has given up
When he might have captured the victor's cup;
And he learned too late when the night came down,
How close he was to the golden crown.

Success is failure turned inside out –
The silver tint of the clouds of doubt,
And you never can tell how close you are,
It may be near when it seems afar;
So stick to the fight when you're hardest hit –
It's when things seem worst,

You must not quit.

INTRODUCTION

LEARNING TO SPEAK THE LANGUAGE OF SUCCESS

When I was growing up, one of my father's favorite sayings was, "The Kennedys didn't get where they are by being born Kennedys, they got there by being raised Kennedys."

He is from a generation of Americans that view the Kennedy family as the epitome of success – Joseph Kennedy, Sr. was the grandson of immigrants who amassed enormous wealth, then saw one son become a Senator, another the Attorney General and a third the President of the United States. Their respective fates notwithstanding, my dad believed that Joe and his sons got to where they were by being trained since birth in the subtle arts of business and politics. Maneuvering through the corporate world and the government was second nature to those men. It came to them as easily as a language they naturally spoke, because they were raised "speaking" Success.

The irony is that my father recognized this fact, but couldn't teach those skills to his own kids. I think he would have liked to pass the talent on, but he just didn't have the experience, and it didn't come naturally to him either. My grandfather was a wonderful man, but not a particularly skilled businessman and not savvy at getting his way against more formidable foes. I have no idea what his parents were like, but I'd venture to say, they weren't master strategists in the finer craft of self-advancement, either. They simply were not Kennedys.

So, my dad stumbled into the corporate world as an engineer, not fluent in the workplace ways that ensure easy progress towards the upper echelons, and I entered the professional ranks the same way – needing to figure out for myself how successful people behave: what was and wasn't acceptable, how to present myself and my ideas, even how to dress and who to spend time with. Nothing came naturally, and I got it wrong more often than I would have liked.

If you weren't raised in an environment where you were groomed for success since birth, how could it possibly come naturally to you? Success is not solely reserved for those who were "raised Kennedy," but it is much easier for them, at least at the outset. They already understand what needs to be done, how to behave, what responses in what situations lead to the most desirable outcomes.

For the rest of us, we need to learn how to be successful step-by-step, the way you'd learn any language that wasn't spoken in your home. Success is achievable, and if you treat it like a foreign language that you have to master, the pursuit of it can be much less daunting.

Many people come from backgrounds where ambition, or any attempt at success, is viewed with suspicion, as if you're trying to make yourself better than others, particularly your family, heritage or culture, or be something you're not. For most of human history, there was no such thing as upward mobility, except possibly by marriage. The servant class was always the servant class, and for self-preservation, they trained their children not to want more, not to aspire to anything greater, because it would only lead to disappointment, or worse.

Caste systems have existed for thousands of years, and in many places still do. This means that not only are children raised without the necessary lessons in success, but are actively discouraged from even trying to reach higher than their birthright. Institutions that have a vested interest in keeping the masses in the trenches send the message that ambition is bad, even evil. Then that message gets passed down through generations to the serving classes, while other families, like the Kennedys, are taught at the dinner table how to strive, achieve and prevail.

If you were on the receiving end of negative messages about ambition in your youth, or even now, block them out of your mind. They no longer apply to you. You deserve to pursue success. Don't let others prevent you from achieving what could and should be yours. If you have a desire to be successful at *anything*, there is no reason not to work towards all of your goals. Let others manage their own feelings, not yours.

This book is structured to make you fluent in Success by the last page. Read all of the chapters and do all of the exercises. Discover how to define success and achieve it on your own. You'll learn how to avoid "Failure Spirals" and acknowledge your achievements, and how to show the world you're successful.

Treat this as you would any other textbook. Follow the lessons, do the work, highlight what's important to you, and make notes. Don't be afraid to go back and recheck areas you may have forgotten or just need to review again. Put each exercise into practice immediately, and chart your results. If you have setbacks, don't give up!

How many years have you been on this planet? You've had that long to become the person you are, so give yourself enough time to become the person you want to be.

Believe me, you can be fluent in the language of Success, even if you weren't raised like a Kennedy.

CHAPTER ONE

MY JOURNEY

I wound up in law school at U.C., Berkeley by accident, having been unable to secure a spot in an Economics Ph.D. Program my senior year of college. I knew within the first two weeks that I didn't belong there and after finishing that first year with decent enough grades for my next move, I left school to work a series of hourly jobs while applying for Ph.D. programs in my chosen field, Environmental Economics.

I got into the Agricultural & Resource Economics program at Berkeley, and since it was Berkeley, I re-admitted to the law school as well. In 1995, having completed all of the course work for my law degree and a Masters of Science, I decided not to finish my doctoral dissertation and to instead start practicing law.

My first job was in the Business & Technology practice of Brobeck, Phleger & Harrison, a large San Francisco firm at the epicenter of the dotcom boom. It was an insane time to be a young associate in the B&T group. We had just lost Netscape as a client because the partner who represented the company underestimated its importance, both to the firm and to the market, and our department was hemorrhaging attorneys who were leaving to form their own law firms, go to other big firms, or go in-house with high-tech clients.

The work was crazy and the hours even crazier. The first day of 1996 that I didn't go into the office was the Fourth of July. My first Initial Public Offering (IPO) was a deal I wound up running when the senior associate quit. The client was OzEmail, an Australian company going public on the NASDAQ, and no other attorney in my firm had ever done a deal like this for an Australian company, so I was on my own to figure it out, which I somehow managed to do.

My second IPO was E*TRADE.

I had been practicing law for exactly five months when I became one of two lead associates on the E*TRADE offering. Later, I learned that my involvement had been the subject of a bet between the company's CEO, Christos Cotsakos, and the partner I worked for, Tom Bevilacqua. Christos didn't want a first year associate on the team, and Tom wagered my portion of the bill that once it was done, Christos wouldn't have a complaint. Tom won.

I could have easily spent the rest of my career at Brobeck, except I was horrible at office politics and political maneuverings among the partners in our group left me in an untenable position. I regularly worked with five other associates, but in the first three months of 1997, four quit and one got fired. I was the last to hold out, lasting only two months after the fifth departure. With hours drying up and deals taken out from under me, I finally gave in…or gave out, depending on how you look at it. I quit.

I was almost immediately hired by Wilson, Sonsini, Goodrich and Rosati, the pre-eminent Silicon Valley law firm, but instead of starting right away, I took a 2-month hiatus to regroup and figure out what the hell had just happened. As a result, I never made it to Wilson Sonsini. Three weeks into my sabbatical, I started my own consulting firm.

Goalkeeper Consulting specialized in preparing business plans and venture capital presentations for start-up companies. It was a middling success. I got to the point where I was covering my monthly bills and paying down some of the debt I had accrued. I had twelve clients and by the summer of 1998, one of them was ready to start meeting with investment banks.

One banker I knew to call was Richard Char, a former Wilson Sonsini partner who had worked opposite me on that first IPO in Australia. He had just been named the head of Technology Banking at a small investment bank in San Francisco.

Richard met with my client and me, made it halfway through their presentation, thanked them for coming, and asked me to stay behind for a moment after ushering them out the door. Once they left the room, Richard offered me a job as an investment banker. I didn't want to roll up my consultancy, but the offer was too good to pass up. Two weeks later, on a Friday, I signed my contract with Cowen & Company to start a new career as a corporate finance associate. What I didn't know was how many other contracts were being signed in that office at that very moment.

Monday morning, when I showed up for my new job, the announcement was made that over the weekend, Cowen & Company had been acquired by the French bank, Société Générale. The new owners were effusive in their public affirmation that nothing would change. They explained that they had "acquired Cowen for its assets and its assets were its people." That sentiment lasted a week.

The following Monday, the employees of the newly named SG Cowen were all introduced to our new CEO, new CFO, and the new heads of Research, Marketing, and Banking. My mentor and champion, Richard Char, was gone in eight months. I lasted 2 months longer.

That's not to say that I didn't do well at SG Cowen. I actually did, but investment banking was not for me. Investment bankers do not contribute to the economic well being of our country. They build nothing, manufacture nothing, and do nothing to increase the size of the economic pie. What they do is rearrange the pieces of the pie and take seven percent for themselves. I couldn't accept that my work had so little value, so in early 1999, I left and became the V.P. of Business Development at a promising Internet start-up that was far ahead of its time. We did online streaming of live sporting events – long before broadband was widely available in the home market.

As the company struggled to stay afloat, I got a call one day that my mother had been rushed to the hospital with a brain tumor. That call, and some other personal upheavals, triggered a difficult six weeks for me. The upshot was that I quit my job, sold my house and car, gave away all my furniture, and with two suitcases and a dog, moved back to Indiana to take care of my mom. It was the summer of 2000. I had been out of school for five years.

It's funny what you discover when you take the time to tell a story like this. I had never put all of this together in one sitting, but now I'm realizing that Goalkeeper Consulting lasted for ten months, my tenure at SG Cowen lasted ten months, and I was at the start-up for ten months. Maybe ten months was how long it took me to realize a thing wasn't working and move on.

Or, more likely, it was just a giant coincidence.

Furthering the coincidence, I spent the next ten months in Indiana with my mom, not so much to provide medical care, but more for emotional support. The tumor was benign, but it was also one-third of her brain weight, so after it was removed, she had to work to rebuild some cognitive functions that we've all taken for granted since childhood.

The biggest challenge was accepting that at 60 years old, after having worked since she was 14, she would not be able to return to her job, or any job. However, by May of 2001, after traveling extensively and learning how to relax and enjoy not having to be anywhere or answer to anyone, my fully-recovered mom turned to me one day and said, "I can't imagine ever having to go back to work."

That's when I knew it was time to head back to California, which I had come to consider home. In my absence, however, the Internet bubble had burst, and there were no jobs for me to go back to. I was living off the proceeds from the sale of my house, which would last another two years if managed very carefully, so I decided that instead of returning to the San Francisco Bay Area, I'd head to Los Angeles and make my living writing movies – something I had no experience doing or even training for. Insane, I know.

I only knew one person in LA, a friend from law school whose couch I camped on for three weeks. I eventually found a place in a pricey part of town that put me in close proximity to both studios and people working in the business. To live there, I had to do something I'd sworn never to do again – I got roommates. It was a total re-start, like being right out of school, broke and hustling… and I loved it.

I wrote three screenplays and they all sucked. I know this because my next-door neighbor worked in development at Dreamworks, Steven Spielberg's film studio, and he put my scripts in for coverage (the studio evaluation process) and the readers could not have hated them more. Based on the coverage reports they wrote, reading my scripts seemed to make them angry and they let it show. This was a tremendous gift. As great as it is to be told you're wonderful at something, it is far more helpful to be told candidly that you need a lot of improvement.

So I decided it would be a good idea to learn how to write. I chose Ron Suppa's "Introduction to Screenwriting" class at the UCLA Extension because it met twice a week instead of once and I was in a hurry. Ron also had some negative evaluations online from students who found him to be "too honest" critiquing their work – just the professor I was looking for! In the six weeks, I outlined and started writing "PR," a story I wanted to tell about how the public relations industry controls our news media. Class finished, I completed the script, showed it to a few people, and my whole life changed.

Here's the way you know whether a script is good or not – did the person who just read it give it back? It doesn't matter what words are coming out of their mouths ("This is so good," "I love your characters and the dialogue," "This is one of the best things I've ever read..."), as soon as they hand it back to you, you know it sucks. Because when it doesn't suck, they don't give it back to you. What they say is, "Can I show this to my friend, the producer/agent/manager/etc.?"

There are only two ways to get ahead in Hollywood – you have talent, or you have access to talent. The great majority of people don't have talent, so they advance their careers by attaching themselves to other people or their work. I knew "PR" was special because the first nine people who read it all tried to attach themselves to it.

From that script, I met managers and got tons of meetings, including one with Matt Bierman, then a production executive at Phoenix Pictures. Matt brought me in to pitch an adaptation they were developing with Joel Schumacher attached to direct. It took weeks to set up the meeting, during which time I worked my ass off on the pitch, but Joel hired another writer before we met. To this day I'm amazed at what happened next, especially now that I know so much more about how this town – "Hollywood" – works. Because I had put in so much time and effort, Matt forced Joel to meet with me anyway and, shockingly, he agreed.

I drove to Joel's house in Bel Air, a hilltop hideaway behind an ivy-covered gate. I went in, spent an hour and a half chatting and pitching, got back in my car, and immediately called my manager. He told me he had an important call on the other line and to call back in five minutes. I was so annoyed. What could be more important than what

I had to tell him about how my pitch meeting with the famous director had gone? But I didn't have good cell phone coverage anyway, so I waited until I reached Sunset Blvd. and called back.

The call on the other line was Matt Bierman.
He had just spoken to Joel.
I had the job!

Working on that movie was an education. I learned some lessons the hard way (more about that later), but it got me into the Writers Guild (the WGA, the union that represents screenwriters) and launched a career that included writing for Catherine Zeta-Jones, Ice Cube, and others.

What followed was a whirlwind of screenwriting success and failure. I signed with Creative Artists (then the most powerful agency in the industry), then with Paradigm, a smaller agency I thought would be a better fit, switched managers and got married, walked the picket line with the rest of my union during a protracted strike, began directing, made a few short films plus 49 commercials and Public Service Announcements on behalf of political causes and candidates I believe in. Ultimately I realized that to have a sustained career as a writer, I simply couldn't depend on anyone else to hire me or buy my scripts. I had to write something else, and it had to be something that mattered – to me and the world.

I wrote *Happiness as a Second Language* in the summer of 2010, and was immediately signed by a prominent literary agent in the non-fiction space. We spent two years chasing traditional publishing contracts that never appealed to me, and when my contract with the agent expired, I leapt on the learning curve of independent publishing. At the same time, I launched my speaking career with a signature talk, *How Women Can Succeed in the Workplace (Despite Having 'Female Brains')*, which is also now a bestselling book.

I spoke at schools, conferences and networking groups, I gave workshops for entrepreneurs, helping them stay positive, move forward, and avoid falling into the "Failure Spiral." I created a series of workshops focused on helping companies lower costs, increase returns, and maximize profits by making happiness in the workplace a priority, and I developed a program to train others how to be "Happiness Facilitators" in their communities.

Some of the lessons and techniques from those talks and workshops are woven throughout this book, and there are several more "..as a Second Language" books on the horizon, as I now own the trademark on the use of "...as a Second Language" for self-help and personal growth titles. I guess not getting hired as a screenwriter for the past few years has paid off. Who could have guessed?

So, in short, I'm successful. In some instances, I fell into opportunities that I made the most of. Other times, I chose fields where I could excel, did the work, and built the skills to succeed. In still other cases, I found I couldn't achieve the outcomes I wanted and changed direction. Some things came naturally, but most times it was the result of major, often painful, trial-and-error.

The chapters that follow share the lessons I've learned. As with all "...as a Second Language" books, this is not an afternoon read, but rather a textbook that gives back only as much you put into it. Always be honest with yourself, see what works for you and what doesn't, and never give up on being a success. It is within your reach.

CHAPTER TWO

THE MANY DEFINITIONS OF SUCCESS

Comment allez-vous?
Je suis bien.

Wie geht es Ihnen?
Ich bin fein.

你好吗?
我很好.

The most rudimentary conversation in any language starts with someone asking "How are you?" and you responding with some variation of, "I'm fine."

Stop for a moment and imagine that instead of responding with, "I'm fine," your response is "I'm successful." In fact, say it out loud to yourself right now – "I'm successful." Go ahead...say it.

What does that feel like? Does it feel exciting or does it feel like a lie? Does it feel like you're speaking a foreign language because you aren't 100% sure what the word means? As long as *success* is some amorphous concept that you cannot nail down or measure, how will you ever feel truly successful?

Let's start by defining success. There's a story I first saw in 1996, which makes its way around the Internet every few years, that takes on this challenge of how we define success for ourselves. I've searched extensively to find the original author, but it's been attributed to so many that I'm including it here without attribution. Most appearances of it are followed by the words, "author unknown," and so will this one.

The Fisherman and the Executive

author unknown

There was once an executive who was vacationing by the beach in a small fishing village.

As she sat on the sand, she saw a fisherman rowing a boat towards the shore having caught quite a few big fish. The executive was impressed and asked the fisherman, "How long does it take you to catch so many fish?"

The fisherman replied, "Oh, just a short while."

"Then why don't you stay longer at sea and catch even more?" She asked.

"This is enough to feed my whole family, give some to friends, and sell a few in the market." the fisherman said.

The executive then asked, "So, what do you do for the rest of the day?"

The fisherman replied, "Well, I usually wake up early in the morning, go out to sea and catch a few fish, then go back and play with my children for the rest of the morning. We eat a big lunch as a family, then I take a nap with my wife. When evening comes, I join my buddies in the village for a drink — we play guitar, sing and dance through the night."

The executive immediately saw the flaw in the fisherman's lifestyle.

"I could help you to become a more successful person," she shared. "From now on, you should spend all day at sea and try to catch as many fish as possible. When you have saved enough money, you could buy a bigger boat and catch even more fish. Soon you will be able to afford to buy more boats, set up your own production plant for canning, and a distribution network. By then, you will have moved out of this small village to a big city, where you can build an office to manage your other branches."

The fisherman continues, "And how long will that take?"

"Not more than 15 or 20 years. And when the time is right, you can sell the company and you will be rich."

The fisherman asks, "And after that?"

The executive says, "After that, you can retire, you can move to a nice house by a small fishing village, wake up early in the morning, catch a few fish, then return home to play with your grandchildren, eat a big lunch, have a nice afternoon nap with your wife, and when evening comes, you can join your buddies for a drink, play the guitar, sing and dance through the night. You will truly be a success!"

The fisherman smiled, thanked the executive for her thoughts, and went home to play with his children, eat a big lunch and nap with his wife.

This story always shows up on some business blog or happiness website to remind people to enjoy the life they have, live simply, and see the success in their everyday lives. After all, by the executive's definition, the fisherman was already a success.

But what if, when the fisherman asked, "And after that?" the executive said, "After that, you will have created jobs for thousands of people, provided healthy food for millions who might not have access to fresh fish, and built a company that will guarantee employment and security for your children and their children for generations to come."

Now does the fisherman seem so wise and the executive so superficial?

Does this definition of success seem more attractive? To have created a lasting legacy that leaves the world in a better place than before you arrived? Or is it more successful to enjoy your time on the planet to its fullest only while you are here?

Neither definition of success is more "right" than the other. They are simply different views of what success means to different people. The challenge for you is to examine your goals, your desires, your aspirations, and your abilities, then figure out how you will know when you can honestly respond to the question, "How are you?" with the answer, "I'm successful."

I include "abilities" in the list above because success depends on setting yourself up for realistic outcomes, and developing the skills you need to get to your defined level of success. "You can do anything you set your mind to!" is a great mantra and a nice bumper sticker, but if you decide you want to be an Olympic swimmer and you never learn how to swim, it's not going to happen!

This may sound like a joke, but how many people do you know who claim to want something then take no steps to develop the foundation to get it? I wrote three terrible screenplays before I decided to take a class on screenwriting, and it wasn't until after I applied those lessons in my writing that I started selling scripts. Knowing what you can and can't do, what you are willing to work on and what is beyond your ability is extremely important. Again, this is an area where you have to be relentlessly honest with yourself.

Mark Cuban, a very successful businessman, has a great take on this. He observes: "For years, people have been saying 'Follow your passion, follow your passion.' That won't get you anywhere. Follow your effort. Look at what you actually spend time doing and pursue that, because that is what you really care about."

If you think you are passionate about art, but spend all your free time reading mystery novels instead of painting, sculpting or taking classes, then maybe art is not where you should focus your quest for success. Maybe you should think about being a mystery novel blogger or book reviewer, or even becoming a mystery writer yourself.

Some might say that if you don't have the money for art supplies or classes, you can't put your effort there. However, if you really want to pursue art, you could put your effort into getting the resources you need – earning a little extra money, finding free classes, volunteering at an arts program. When something is the true target of your quest for success, you will find a way to get there.

Success is an outcome, not a process.

I'm a working screenwriter and a member of the Writers Guild of America. I've been hired to write screenplays for producers and studios, developed television shows for and with big stars. I've been represented by some of the biggest agencies and managers in the industry, but as of the writing of this book, none of my work has been produced, aside from short works that I've produced myself.

So am I a successful screenwriter? That depends on your definition of successful, and for everyone in the entertainment industry, it's different.

I have a very close friend who sold a script and it got made as a low-budget, independent movie (so she did not get into the Writers Guild), but she never sold another script. She went on to become a prolific entertainment journalist.

In my mind, she is a successful screenwriter. In her mind, she is not.

Many would say I am successful because I've earned good money, had impressive representation, got into the union, and worked for accomplished producers, directors, and actors. However, I have always defined success in this business as having your work produced. That is what my friend has achieved, and I have not. By my definition, she is a successful screenwriter and I am not.

Still, if I choose to switch paths and pursue a different career (something we'll discuss in Chapter Four – changing direction towards more success), I will look back on my time spent in this job and won't think I failed as a screen-writer. I just do not yet think that I'm a success, because I have not yet reached my desired outcome. Remember that not reaching all of your goals is not failure. You are either still in pursuit of success, or you have shifted your goals. The only failure is sticking with the same thing, year after year, with no advancement or growth. Thomas Edison famously said, "I have not failed. I've just found 10,000 ways that won't work."

Once I reach my desired outcome, and can honestly say, "I'm successful," there will be other work to do, and new goals to reach, but I will have succeeded in achieving that outcome. For each individual, the definition is different, but it is your definition that matters for you.

Don't forget that success is also defined in different ways for different areas of our lives. Sometimes this puts goals in conflict with one another. If a salesman defines career success as being the top ranking salesman in his region (requiring extensive travel and long hours), and if he defines personal success as being happily married and involved in his kids' lives, it may be impossible to achieve both goals at the same time. This is where life requires us to prioritize.

Again, there is no right or wrong answer. You might be thinking, "How can anyone say it's better to be the top salesman in a region than to spend more time with your children?" But that opinion might not consider the long-term results of each choice. If it takes one year of sacrificing time with his children to reach the top, and that leads to a job with greater freedom, less travel and more flexibility, then might that be the better choice? On the other hand, if a family decides that they'd prefer to have time together rather than material rewards, then perhaps achieving that is the more successful choice.

Think about the various definitions of a successful career, which could be any of the following:

1. I keep the same job until retirement.

2. I become nationally recognized in my field.

3. I earn enough to support myself.

4. I never burn a bridge.

5. I create something that changes the world.

6. I get filthy rich.

7. I leave work every day as happy or happier than when I arrived.

8. I have plenty of free time to travel and pursue my hobbies.

9. I am always learning new things.

10. I have a large workforce that reports to me.

11. I am completely self-sufficient.

12. I work from home.

13. I change careers every five years.

14. I have the largest office in the building.

15. I never set foot in an office.

EXERCISE:

RIGHT NOW, TAKE OUT a piece of paper or open a new screen and write down your definition of success in your career. Separately, write your definition of success in your personal life. **These must be your own definitions for yourself.**

IF YOUR MOTHER TOLD you that you have to earn six figures to really make it, but that is not important to you, don't include it in your definition. However, if that is important, include it!

REMEMBER, THESE DEFINITIONS ARE for your eyes only, so don't censor yourself because of what others might think or judge.

If this feels difficult or challenging, here's a guideline – look around you at the people you regard as successful and those you regard as unsuccessful in their careers and lives. What makes you think that way? What have they achieved or failed to achieve that determines your view? This is not about comparing yourself or your progress to them, it's about using others' successes and failures as examples to help you create your own definition of success.

Also, remember that definitions of success change over time. Don't set goals today that you don't really want at this stage in your life, or that you will not actually work to achieve.

Right now, your definition of career success might be, "Work just enough hours every day in a stress-free job to pay my bills and have the rest of the time free to surf or play video games." If that's where you are, admit it and make it happen.

When you fulfill that goal and you want more, or when that level of career success prevents you from being able to reach your goals for personal success (such as, "travel to a foreign country every year," or, "get married and have 2.3 children"), then come back to this book and go through all of the exercises again, focusing on your new definition. Remember, success is all about how you define it for yourself.

To help, here are my definitions, which are probably different from everyone else's in the fields in which I work. I also want to point out that many people believe career success includes having a job that makes them feel happy, fulfilled and accomplished, and I agree. Those are not included in my definitions below because I have already chosen careers that do that for me automatically, so my definitions are focused on more tangible, measurable criteria.

1. To be a successful author, I have to earn enough money through book sales to be able to continue to focus my time on writing.

2. To be a successful screenwriter, my work has to be produced (by someone other than me) and appear on a screen where the general public can see it.

3. To be a successful director, I have to get paid to direct.

4. To be a successful speaker, I have to be paid to speak.

5. To be successful in my personal life, I have to make the happiness of the people I love a top priority, which will keep them in my life and make me even happier.

Of the five definitions above, some have already been achieved and some are still on my Goals Calendar (which we cover in Chapter Four).

In the areas where I have already reached what I consider success, I still have further ambitions, and more outcomes to strive for, but I am not going to change my own goal line. I can accurately say, "I am a successful _____," even if I do nothing else in that field.

You may be surprised that my definitions focus so much on generating income, rather than inspiring people with my work, but my work has already reached millions of people. The greatest reward is when readers reach out to tell me how my work touched them, and I experience that every day. A single article I wrote for the Huffington Post had more than two million views, elicited thousands of comments, tens of thousands of shares, hundreds of thousands of "likes" and spawned nearly one hundred blog posts, and I'm very proud of that achievement, but I was not paid to write it, nor for any of the media appearances that followed. For me, consistently getting paid to do something is what delineates a career from a hobby, and I want to be successful in these areas – writing, speaking and screenwriting – as careers. Again, everyone's interpretation of success is different.

These definitions have not been tossed off lightly. They took years to hone. For example, I used to think being a successful author meant getting on bestseller lists and that being a successful screenwriter meant winning an Oscar. But those things are out of my control, and they set me up to fail, to potentially never get there. And to be perfectly honest, they weren't really *my* definitions – they were what I thought the rest of the world believed.

When someone asks, "How are you?" you want to be able to answer honestly with "I'm successful." The easiest way to do that is to define success in specific, personal, achievable ways that you believe, wholeheartedly and without anyone else's opinion clouding your vision. Don't change the definition as you get close to it and don't let anyone else tell you it's wrong. Success is an outcome, and once you define it, you can achieve it.

CHAPTER THREE

THE NUMBERS OF SUCCESS

Uno, dos, tres, cuatro, cinco
Un, deux, trois, quatre, cinq
ichi, ni, san, shi, go

Can you count to five in at least one foreign language? Counting is one of those easy, rote memorization things that we all pick up right away when learning a new language.

So how do you count in the language of Success? It's a little different, but just as easy to learn. In Success, you count by making a list of five things that you accomplished today. Do this daily. Some things may appear on your list every day, and some things will be new from one day to the next.

For me, this habit is one of the greatest legacies of having practiced law. Almost all law firms run on the fuel of billable hours. The more hours the lawyers bill, the more money the firm makes. What this does for young professionals, fresh out of school, is teach an efficiency that many industries don't engender. When you're a first-year associate at a law firm, nothing is worse than being in the office for ten or twelve hours and at the end of the day, discovering that you only billed for four of them.

This happens often in the first six months on the job, until you get into the habit of writing down everything you do as you do it, even things that aren't billable. My time sheets started the minute I sat at my desk, usually with listening to voice mail and checking email (even though there was no client to bill for that time), then, clocking the time, I started on whatever had the top priority that day. If my work got interrupted by a client's call or a partner needing help on another matter, that time was recorded too, even if it was just a five- or ten-minute distraction. Lunch was always written, as were coffee breaks and conversations with colleagues. Every activity noted just so I could see where my time went each day.

My firm billed by the tenth of the hour, which meant tracking the day in six-minute increments, and I was obsessed with not overcharging clients by rounding up to the nearest half or quarter hour. I realize that it's my own peculiar view of money, service, and value that led me to this level of diligence, but that attitude has helped me to develop one of the best habits that I would carry through the rest of my professional life – tracking the time in each day.

The wonderful side effect of this was that as I headed out the door each day (often at 2:00 or 3:00 a.m.), I could look over my time sheets and see just how much I'd gotten done and what still needed finishing. This became one of my favorite little rituals. Now, nearly 20 years later, I can still recall moments of joy on those nights when, exhausted beyond measure, I took that moment to reflect and give myself a little mental reward for being good at my job and providing something of value to the world. It also marked a definitive end to the workday, when I would release my brain from work and head home, clear-headed.

A few years later, when I switched from law to investment banking, I found a markedly different workplace lifestyle – one in which colleagues spent hours in each other's offices talking about basketball or movies before starting work somewhere around 4:00 in the afternoon, or they left in the middle of the day to go test drive new cars before coming back to the office to work late into the night.

I was told that I didn't spend enough "face time" in the office. My boss pointed out that the VPs and senior associates almost never saw me there at 10:00 p.m. or midnight, when most of the other associates and analysts were still toiling away. I told him that I kept a running list of my accomplishments every day, and I'd be happy to match my list against any other person's to see who gets the most work done, but that I wasn't staying late into the night after I'd gotten everything finished by 7:00 p.m. just to be seen. He didn't like my answer, but luckily, his boss was the managing director who had hired me, and as a former attorney himself, was definitely on my side.

(However, if you work at a place that requires "face time," it's a good idea to be there when everyone else is, even if you are better at getting everything accomplished during a more traditional workday. That's just good office politics, and managing that part of your career is as important to your success as doing a good job.)

Tracking your daily accomplishments has real value, which is why it's one of the basic vocabulary lessons in the language of Success. There are many techniques for Counting to Five in Success. Here are just two:

1. Wait until the end of the day and write down the first five things that come to mind, or the five that are most significant.

2. Keep a small notebook with you at all times, and whenever it hits you that you just got something done, whip it out and write it down, which often leads to lists longer than five.

Why do this? Because accomplishments are our mile-markers on the road to success. The more accomplishments you have in your day, the more successful you will feel, and the more you can recognize when you are moving towards the outcomes you desire. This also helps you give yourself an honest assessment of how efficiently you focus your attention and get things done.

We tend to ignore or discount accomplishments throughout the day when we don't track them, and we don't give ourselves credit for "time served." If you have to stretch to come up with five accomplishments at the end of the day, go ahead and include things like, "Responded to Pam's email about lunch," and "Wrapped the present for the baby shower," or even, "Took out the trash."

Why put such trivial things on your list? Because they had to get done and they took up your time. They took time that you might not think was spent on your quest for success, but the truth is, it was.

Performing the necessary tasks of survival is a basic component of being successful in any endeavor. You may be working 15 hours a day, every day, to launch that fabulous design boutique, but you still have to pay your bills, buy groceries, walk the dog, and return your mother's phone calls (at least those last two can be done at the same time). Give yourself credit for doing the little things by including them in your daily accomplishments. This is especially important when you're first striking out on your own and have days on end without good news, feedback, or even the glimmer of a light at the end of the tunnel.

Taking note of your accomplishments is also the best way to avoid the "Failure Spiral." Once things start to feel like they aren't going well, it takes very little to start thinking that they will never go well, and then believing that nothing will ever go well, and finally that everything you're doing is a disaster, that you've made a huge mistake, and that you are a complete failure!

HALT!!!

When these thoughts become overwhelming, it's time to stop and ask yourself, "What have I accomplished today?" Write down at least five things you've done today and do your best to come up with more than five, if you can.

Right now, even as I type this chapter, I'm waiting to hear from two different film directors, one who's reading a television pilot of mine to potentially attach himself to produce and direct (an outcome that could change my life), and another who's reading a book of mine to possibly write an endorsement for the cover. I hate waiting and often find myself falling into the Failure Spiral, second guessing everything I do, re-reading and finding flaws in what I've written, and generally focusing on things other than my success.

Feeling this way cannot change the outcome. It only detracts from my ability to pursue other goals while I wait. So right now, I'm stopping, shooting off a quick Count to Five list, and getting back on track.

Hey… I'm back. It's a little after noon, so let's take a look at what I've accomplished today on my road to career and personal success.

1. I've written half a chapter in the new book (that would be this one…)

2. I had breakfast with my husband (personal success matters, too…)

3. The editor and I locked picture on the short film that I wrote and directed. (Technically that was last night, but since we wrapped at 1:00 a.m., I'm going to give it to myself for today…)

4. I reviewed a composer's website for the short film and listened to all of his music samples, so that I can talk to him about the exact sound I want. (I'd told myself this was just a distraction from writing, but now I realize how valuable and important it was.)

5. I reached out to several contacts to find the rest of the post-production staff (sound editor, color correction, title artist).

6. I posted on the **Happiness as a Second Language Facebook page.**

   [Note: Social media is a necessity to market my books, but it requires a lot of self-discipline to use it judiciously, particularly on a day spent waiting for news. It's so easy to lose an hour scrolling through my timeline, so I force myself to log off Facebook immediately after I make my posts.]

7. I read, replied to, and deleted email in my various inboxes.

So now, it's 12:45 in the afternoon, and I am feeling much more successful than I did just fifteen minutes ago.

While I was doing them, the things listed above felt like worthless distractions, but now I recognize that they are really valid steps towards the outcomes I desire. Yes, I admit that I spent time this morning on non-success endeavors (reading news articles by people who agree with me politically, watching funny videos, leaving feedback for a seller on ebay), but the day no longer feels like it's been thrown away. Stopping to make my Count to Five list has also given me a renewed commitment to make the rest of my workday as productive as possible.

Tonight, my husband and I are going to visit a friend who is fighting a tough battle with leukemia. I'm pretty sure that after this visit, I will not return to writing about the language of Success. Instead, I'll probably turn my attention to writing about Happiness, and how to maintain it in the face of life's toughest challenges, or I may just make dinner for my family and watch *Project Runway* on TV. Given that I'm going to finish this chapter before we leave, I'll give myself credit for accomplishing enough today.

Every day, you have a choice. You can be the lawyer who is in the office for 10 hours and bills nine of them, or you can be the investment banker who works 14 hours a day, stays past midnight every night for a week, and still can't finish building a deal book (which takes about 20 hours of real work) because so much of your time is simply "face time" spent looking at golf catalogues or ordering toys from Amazon. The more you can accomplish each day, the more successful you will feel and be, so accomplish as much as you can, and acknowledge all that you've done.

The point is, whether you track your day in billable hours, make a list at the end of each night, or stop a Failure Spiral by listing as many accomplishments as you can muster, there is no right or wrong way to Count to Five. But don't skip even a single day. One skipped day leads to two skipped days and before long, you've stopped counting in your new language because you've forgotten how to do it.

You may feel silly at first, or feel that you're forcing it. Just don't quit. Eventually, you'll notice that on most days you have a hard time keeping yourself to only five accomplishments. You'll also notice that your lists become more focused on specific success quests and less on the little time-sucking activities and trivial tasks. You'll start to see your success opening right before your very eyes.

POP QUIZ!

Stop reading now. Grab a pen or open a new screen and make a list of five things that you accomplished today. If it's early in the morning, make it five things you accomplished yesterday. Right now. Do it!

1.

2.

3.

4.

5.

Was that easy? I hope so. If it was easy, you are well on your way to being fluent in Success. If it was hard, you're still starting out, but don't worry, it will get easier as you practice.

Or did you skip it and just keep reading? If so, why? Did you have a hard time even coming up with the first one? If you did have a hard time, let's get over that first hurdle. If you can't come up with even a single thing to put on your Count-to-Five list, use this as your first accomplishment today:

1. I read a chapter in a book about Success.

In fact, you're still reading, and that is an accomplishment. It shows a commitment to being more successful, a desire to expand your views, and it's a real activity that will actually get you closer to your goals. Now, think of four more things you've done today that might meet one of those criteria, even if they include small things that aren't directly on your path to success (like taking the cat to the vet or changing your cell phone carrier).

Counting to Five in Success has multiple benefits. It focuses your attention on what you're getting done and where your priorities are. It gives you an honest assessment of what you're not getting done and may want to devote more time to. It gives you credit for all the time spent on your daily tasks, whether on your success journey or not. It can be a signal booster (when you're feeling successful, rattle off a quick list to reinforce the feeling of success) or a signal disruptor (to stop the Failure Spiral).

You may come from a background where you were taught to never relish your own accomplishments, or that no matter what you did, it wasn't good enough. You can overcome those notions and emotions. Pay close attention to how much you really do each day, and allow yourself the freedom and confidence to acknowledge your achievements, even in the smallest of tasks. And if you don't think that you're getting enough done for your own satisfaction, don't worry, Chapter Four is all about how to create and pursue daily, monthly and lifetime goals that are within your reach.

If you think you are successful or you think you are unsuccessful, chances are, you're right. A requirement of being successful is believing that you can be. If you weren't raised speaking Success, practice Counting to Five every day in your new language, and you'll soon develop faith and confidence in your own potential. As you do this more and more, you'll see that what you write or say doesn't matter, so much as the act of doing it. This is why you must do it every day. Like mastering any new language, the Language of Success requires practice and repetition.

CHAPTER FOUR

DAYS OF THE WEEK AND MONTHS OF THE YEAR

Sonntag, Montag, Dienstag, Mittwoch, Donnerstag, Freitag, Samstag

Συνδαυ, Μονδαυ, Τυεσδαυ, Ωεδνεσδαυ, Θυρσδαυ, Φριδαυ, Σατυρδαυ

Март -го февраль -го январь...

One of the early lessons in any foreign language is learning how to say the days of the week and the months of the year.

In Success, the days of the week are spoken through the completion of tasks and the months of the year are used to track your goals, both small and massive. If ambition, commitment and dedication were not part of the language spoken in your home growing up, and do not come naturally to you now, then you must take steps to acquire these traits, by days and months.

How do you get success "by the day?" You do it by announcing to yourself what you will do each day and then doing it.

The surest way to lose momentum is to set yourself up for failure. Don't overburden yourself with tasks you could not possibly complete in the hours in a single day, only to end each day with the feeling that you let yourself down. Decide what you will do each day, write it down, do it, and as you complete and cross off tasks, don't add more.

One of the workshops based on the book, *Happiness as a Second Language,* focuses on building happier workplaces. In this workshop, I meet with employees in the morning and with managers in the afternoon. A common complaint I hear from the employees is that their bosses will start the day saying, "Do A, B and C today," and after the worker has done A and B, the boss changes the agenda and says, "Okay, now do X, Y and Z," without any acknowledgement of what has already been accomplished, or even an explanation of whether C is still on the list. This is called "changing the goal line," and it is the mark of a bad boss.

Don't be your own bad boss. If you have a task to do, give yourself enough time to complete it, recognize when it's done, and give yourself credit for completing the work. Don't pile on more tasks just because you've finished the last one.

But things do change…that's just a fact of life. If you discover that something else is more important or urgent than what you're working on, first take a moment to re-establish what you need to get done today. If the tasks you're setting aside are still critical, put them on a list "to be done later," but remember that they are no longer on today's list.

There is another famous story about a business school professor who walked into class one day with a jar and a box of rocks. He started placing large rocks into the jar until they reached the rim, and asked his class, "Is the jar full?" They all agreed it was full.

Then the professor started putting small pebbles into the jar until they reached the rim. He turned to the class and asked, "Is the jar full?" Some said "No," but many said, "Yes, now it was full." The professor then pulled out a pail of sand and slowly poured it into the jar until it reached the rim and once again asked, "Is the jar full?" At this point, some said "Yes," some said "No," but most remained completely silent, having no idea what the right answer was (and being business students, not willing to risk their grades on getting it wrong again.)

The professor then pulled out a cup of water and slowly dribbled it into the jar as it soaked into the sand. When it reached the rim, he said, "Now the jar is full" The class all breathed a sigh of relief, until he asked, "What does that teach you?"

Most students answered with some form of the statements, "No matter how much you've done, there's always room to do more," or "Don't make judgments about your results without knowing all of the materials you're working with."

The professor shook his head and told them that the real lesson was: "If you want to get the big rocks in, put them in first."

The point of the story is that the big rocks symbolize the things that matter most *to you* – family, health, maybe career and other pursuits, and in life, the big rocks have to come first.

Another way to interpret this, however, is that in business, our schedule (the container in the professor's example) is filled with tasks. The size of the rocks translates into the importance of the tasks. To fill our schedules completely, efficiently, and effectively, we must start with the most important tasks, and fill the gaps in the timeline with progressively less important tasks.

When you speak the language of Success, you have to decide what the "big rocks" are for yourself. Decide what things are most important for you and do them first.

How do you put the "big rocks" first? You decide what they are and you write them down. You make a smart, organized, to-do list.

For example, every day I make a to-do list. In the past, it always included some basic life activities (make dinner, walk the dog), some administrative activity (pay the electric bill, put gas in the car), and at least half a dozen "big rocks" relating to my work, none of which could all be accomplished within the waking hours of that day. At the end of every day, I looked at the things that didn't get crossed off the list and beat myself up a little for not getting it all done.

Once I started speaking Success, I changed my approach to the act of making this list, and that changed the outcome. Now, I start with one big rock (the most critical task to advance my career), and put it on the list, underlined. I *will* get that done today. Then I move to the pebbles (the important things I need to get done to sustain my career). Then comes the sand (everything I want to do, either for my career or for myself, that doesn't necessarily *need* to get done today, but has to get done eventually). Finally, I consider the water (those *nice-to-have* things that I want to do *sometime,* but don't need done by some deadline).

Because I derive pleasure from crossing things off a list, I design mine so that I can cross everything off with time to spare. I include rocks, pebbles, sand, and water. Things that are critical (like proofreading a script); things that are important (and scheduled – like a dentist appointment); and things that are a given (shower, eat lunch). After that, I include things I'd like to do if I have time (a hike with my dog). I put everything on my list so that I give myself credit for all the activities and time in my daily schedule.

You need to decide what are your rocks, your pebbles, your sand, and your water.

This list is the roadmap you follow to keep yourself on track. Ideally, it will be exactly what you look back on and reward yourself for at the end of the day when you Count to Five. That's why you include everything, all the pebbles, sand and water, not just the rocks. You know you have to eat lunch, you know it takes time out of your day (even if you're multitasking while you chew), so put it on the list, and you won't feel like you lost half an hour doing "nothing."

For me, it takes an enormous amount of self-discipline not to be my own bad boss. I always want to add things to my list, especially on days when it doesn't look like anything of value is getting done. But, I get a great sense of accomplishment from crossing everything off, and that's why it's so important to keep my to-do list simple and focused.

When you finish your list, if there's spare time at the end of the day, you have a choice: you can add another task, or you can reward yourself with a little leisure. If you choose your rocks and pebbles carefully, you will complete everything that *needs* to get done every day, without losing your success-driven momentum.

Another reason to make a more comprehensive list, besides that warm feeling of success you get crossing things off, is that it shows you exactly how much you really are doing. If you only have two things on a to-do list, and you don't get to one of them, you can easily slip into a Failure Spiral, even if those two things are really big rocks like: (1) write a business plan, and (2) restructure the accounting system. While those may be the most important things you want to accomplish, they are not the only things you do in your day.

However, if you include everything you do on your list…

1. Go to the gym

2. Eat breakfast

3. Call the insurance company about the car

4. Commute to work

5. Reply to email

6. Read analyst reports and newsletters

7. **Write the marketing section of the Business Plan** (always highlight the big rock)

8. Eat lunch

9. Proofread the marketing section of the Business Plan

10. Come up with the goals of the revamped accounting system

11. Review accounting software proposals

12. Return all phone calls

13. Commute home

14. Prepare dinner

15. Do one load of laundry

16. Watch last night's recorded TV episodes

...then crossing everything off except "Review accounting software proposals" shows you that a lot was done that day – because it was! Even better, if you know the chances of getting to the proposals are slim, don't put it on today's list. Why set yourself up for failure?

As you get better at making this list, you'll see how easy it is to focus on the things you must get done and let go of things that aren't contributing to your success.

Learning the days of the week in the language of Success is one of those skills that requires repetition, but soon becomes second nature. Each day is a new chance to practice.

Learning the months of the year in Success takes you from the short term to the long term, and forces even greater honesty and accountability. In Chapter Two, you wrote your definitions for career and personal success, and now it's time to start pursuing them.

Look carefully at each of your definitions of success, and write down the steps you need to take to reach those definitions. If you have no idea what steps might be required, then you have a very easy goal for your First Month of Success – determine what it takes to be successful according to your own definitions.

Is that too esoteric or does it seem not helpful? If so, try harder and really put in the effort to figure out how to succeed. This part takes real work! Perhaps the very thing you want to do has been done before by someone else, maybe even several people. Maybe one of them has shared his or her journey with the world, in an autobiography, a how-to book, a magazine article, or maybe even in a celebrity interview. Do a little bit of research, and begin to make your own list of steps to follow.

Is your definition of career success starting and running your own business? Here's a list of very broad goals you might start with, a list you can get from a business website, an online course, the Small Business Administration, or any basic business book in the library.

1. Decide what product or service you want to sell

2. Choose a business structure (for example, corporation, LLC, sole proprietor)

3. Secure the capital to get started

4. Make a plan to market your product or service

5. Build or rent facilities

6. Hire the necessary employees

7. Begin manufacturing your product or developing your service

8. Offer it to the market

Within each of those broad strokes are potentially dozens, if not hundreds, of specific objectives, that you can list, prioritize, and start pursuing on a monthly basis.

You may think you're set for #1 above – you already know exactly what product you're going to sell, but before moving to #2, maybe one of your monthly goals should be to research competing products and determine how to differentiate yours from others. If you truly believe there are no competing products in the market, then you might want to know why that is. It may be that you've come up with the greatest invention since the ballpoint pen, and you'll be the first ever to sell it, but it may also be that there is no market for what you want to sell. This is an important thing to know before you spend time, money and energy pursuing an unattainable goal…an effort that cannot result in success, no matter how much work you put into it.

Years ago, I created and ran a non-profit program in the Silicon Valley called "The Dry Run." We gave early stage start-up companies the opportunity to show their pitches to Venture Capitalists for the purpose of getting unbiased, professional feedback in a non-fundraising arena.

At least half the companies who presented could not adequately describe their competition, and at least half of those said, "We have no competition," which got them roasted by our VC consultants. Those startups were lucky. If they had said they had no competition in an actual fundraising pitch, the real VCs would have stopped listening. No one would pay attention to anything else they had to say. If you don't understand your competition, you are destined to fail, or at least struggle greatly, and that's just one of the things you need to know to get a new business started.

The point here is that there are always many small steps to take within each of the larger steps towards success, and that can feel overwhelming, especially if you weren't raised with the mindset to deal with it. The simple way to overcome this potential obstacle is to have specific, attainable monthly goals. You have to determine for yourself when you've achieved each smaller goal and move on to the next until you reach your main goal on the road to your defined level of success.

In my quest to become a successful author, one of my broad goals was to learn how to market a book without a publisher or publicist on the team. This was broken down into multiple educational objectives, so I began taking classes, workshops, and online webinars. Eventually, I reached the point of diminishing returns. I recognized that I'd learned all I could, one more webinar was not going to teach me anything I didn't already know, and it was time to move to the next step: actually marketing the book myself.

This is a scary leap of faith – to say that you have researched enough and are ready to take action, but action is required for all successful pursuits.

The months in the language of Success start with taking your definitions of success from Chapter Two and breaking them down into 8-10 broad steps that might take weeks, months or even years to achieve (for example, "graduate from college"), then breaking the steps down into manageable monthly objectives for yourself. If you are unsure what steps are required, then your first month's goal is to learn what they are.

Don't try to do this all in one day. "Learn all the steps I need to succeed" doesn't belong on a single daily task list – a smaller task might be, "Go on the Internet or to the library and find the four best books about my chosen field." You're also not going to read all four books in a day, but you could read them all in a month if you make one of your smaller objectives to read one book each week.

Each month, you need to have actionable goals with measurable outcomes. Once you have your broad steps and sub-steps outlined, you can make a plan for each month. Prioritize your goals (decide which rocks to tackle and when), then for each month, write down "This month I will…"

You can put this plan anywhere – in a notebook, on a white board, on your computer or smart phone, on a sheet of paper taped to the refrigerator – but wherever you put it, make sure it's easy to see while you're prioritizing your daily tasks. Each day you should work towards your monthly goals, and each month should reflect on the progress you've made towards your defined success.

An old Chinese proverb says, "A journey of a thousand-miles begins with a single footstep." Breaking your journey down into smaller and smaller steps lets you see how attainable it is. That's the whole purpose of defining success for yourself, breaking it down into broad sections, breaking those sections down into specific monthly goals, and pursuing those goals in your daily tasks.

There are two more reasons to learn the days and months in the language of Success.

The first is to keep yourself on target, and ruthlessly block out tempting distractions. I'm not talking about the hour you might spend each day chatting on social media (although, unless you're marketing or chatting with potential associates, you might want to think about installing a social media time-limiter in your browser). What I'm talking about is the three weeks you spend on some tangential project that is loads of fun, but doesn't contribute to your success, and doesn't give any value toward accomplishing your goal.

When I was hired for my first screenwriting job, I was admitted into the Writers Guild of America, an enormous accomplishment. I immediately joined committees and started planning educational events and doing all sorts of work for the WGA that put me in touch with some of the most successful screenwriters in the industry. Yes, I was networking, but as any working writer can tell you, networking with other screenwriters isn't exactly the way to get ahead when you're just starting out (as opposed to networking with producers, studio executives, agents and other people who actually hire and represent writers). But it felt GREAT! I was so involved!

I was good at planning and producing events, and everyone treated me with so much respect. My name was in WGA publications, and I did get a meeting or two with some amazing writers, but that wasn't why I moved to Hollywood. Luckily, David Balkan, a seasoned television writer with a long and prosperous career, saw what was going on and took me aside one day and said, "Valerie, don't confuse volunteering for the Guild with having a writing career."

He was so right! Had I taken the time to stop and define success for myself, I would have seen that I was not on the path to it. Had I done the research to break my plans down into broad goals and smaller steps, I would have seen that being "the Guild Girl" (as one friend referred to me) was not on that list.

I'm not saying volunteering is bad. It's wonderful and rewarding, and I still do a great deal of it in my leisure time, which is not my career. Volunteering at the WGA is not one of my success steps, and with that awareness, I devote an appropriate amount of time to it.

On this same point, I have several friends who moved to Los Angeles to pursue acting careers, and by their definition of success, they want to get paid to act in film and television. Yet they all audition for, get cast in, and spend weeks rehearsing and performing in stage plays, a giant waste of time for anyone seriously pursuing film and television acting work in Hollywood. They are not doing Broadway shows or prestigious regional theater. These are generally unpaid roles in 99-seat theaters, some in church basements and above bowling alleys. They beg their friends to come, but they'll never be seen by anyone with the power to give them paid work in film or television.

I get it. It feels good to be on stage and flex those acting muscles, and it's far more rewarding than driving an hour each way for an audition and two callbacks just to be the person sitting next to the star at a lunch counter saying, "Pass the salt." But this is the difference between a hobby and a career. If doing experimental theater in union-waiver houses is how an actor chooses to spend her time, rather than taking classes, working in short films, attending casting director workshops and going to events and seminars where there is a chance to meet producers, directors, managers and agents, then acting is her hobby, not a career.

Does that seem cruel? It may be, but it is also 100% honest, which is a baseline requirement for any pursuit of success. This leads to the second reason to learn how to say the days and months in the language of Success – knowing when to end a particular pursuit and move on.

Changing Direction is NOT Failure

You may find that, after you've done everything right and according to plan, you are still not where you want to be. This could be because what you want has changed or because the success you're pursuing depends too heavily on factors beyond your control and thus unlikely to materialize.

When you've set your goals and objectives, achieved the monthly goals and completed daily tasks, and you can count your accomplishments every day, but you still have not reached success, it is perfectly okay to change direction. Changing direction is not failure. NOTE: You may have just skipped right past that last sentence without really absorbing it, but it's pretty important, so I'll repeat it: CHANGING DIRECTION IS NOT FAILURE.

Others may want to spin it as failure, or you may fear they are saying it behind your back, but so what? Deciding that a particular path is not going to be part of your future is one of the best decisions you can make in order to actually achieve real success.

I have so many friends who came to Los Angeles to be writers, make-up artists, actors, directors and producers, and after giving it a solid try, chose to go follow different paths – teaching, medicine, carpentry, real estate, the list goes on and on. Today, most of these people are successful. I never think of them them as having failed. What I see are people who chose a career, took steps to make that career happen, reached a point where it was no longer fun or feasible to stay on that path, and moved on to better opportunities.

Not everyone sees it that way, but those who want to pass judgment are not the ones who determine your success – you are!

One friend who, by all external measures, was a successful actor – he had an agent, you've seen him on television shows and in commercials, he auditioned regularly, and won coveted roles – realized that it just wasn't fun anymore. He was making good money, but most of it was for saying the equivalent of, "Pass the salt," so he changed direction and started his own design business. Now he is incredibly successful and – more importantly – extremely happy.

Happiness and success go hand-in-hand. If you've defined success as earning a million dollars a year, and you've done that, but at the expense of your health, your family, your social life, and all your free time, are you really successful? The answer here is, "Yes!" Success is all about how you define it for yourself, and if that paycheck is your highest reward, it's not anyone else's business to say whether that is the right metric or not.

If, however, you achieve your defined level of success and discover that you're miserable, don't be afraid to change your definition. Choosing to change is never failing, it's deciding, which we will see in Chapter Seven is the absolute baseline for achieving success. Knowingly staying on a path that *cannot* lead you to where you want to be is failing, especially if the commitment to this wrong direction is based on fear of change or concern with what others will say or think.

I dropped out of law school after my first year because I hated it and knew I didn't want to be a lawyer. Circumstances led me back two years later, and I discovered a great love for practicing law. That love could never have materialized if I had been too concerned with pleasing others and too worried about what they thought of me to ever leave in the first place.

A week after the new semester started for my former classmates, when everyone was still discovering that I was not returning, a friend invited me to go to a party that he promised me, emphatically, was not a law school party. We walked in and not only was everyone there a student at Berkeley Law, they were all from the same small section I was assigned to during the previous year. I had to spend the entire evening in one conversation after another explaining why I was no longer a law student.

It was one of the most difficult nights of my life. It was also my 23rd birthday. Had I known in advance that I would have a night that uncomfortable and embarrassing, I probably would have just stayed in school. But guess what? I survived. And after that night, I never once regretted my decision.

It takes enormous strength and immense self-awareness to know what path you want to be on, how far you can get on that path (which may be far beyond whatever you think your limit is), and when to stick with it or shift focus to a different definition of success or a new set of goals.

But, don't worry, you have all the tools you need.

Here are the steps to become conversational in the language of Success:

1. Define success for yourself.

2. Research how others got there.

3. Break the journey down into 8-10 big steps.

4. Break each of those steps down into 3-20 sub-steps.

5. Make those sub-steps your monthly goals (choose 3-6 per month to pursue, more if you have the time and inclination).

6. With your monthly goals as your guide, create daily task lists that force you to move forward in pursuit of those goals.

7. At the end of each month, do a thorough self-assessment of how far you got, how many goals you achieved, and how accomplished and successful you feel.

8. Write your goals for the next month.

9. Don't let small setbacks or bad months derail your pursuit. Everybody misses the target now and then.

10. Just remember, in baseball, if you hit three out of ten pitches (meaning you miss 70% of the time), you are enormously successful. Keep that in mind as you swing for the fences.

11. Check in with yourself often to see if what you're doing is making you happy, fulfilled, and motivated to reach higher.

12. Don't let anyone else control your decisions. If you have to change direction, do so boldly and without fear or apology.

13. Decide for yourself.

That's what native speakers of Success do.

CHAPTER FIVE

COLORS

Rouge, Jaune, Bleu
Vermelho, Amarelo, Azul
Rot, Gelb, Blau

It's easy to learn the primary colors in a foreign language, but how do you convey the subtleties of crimson versus garnet? Golden or mustard? Teal, aqua or sea-foam? To be truly fluent, you have to get past the basic colors and be able to discuss a whole variety of shades.

Shading in the language of Success is about how you present information about yourself and your accomplishments. You can shade things brightly or darkly, shiny or muted, sparkling or dull, all with your choice of language.

How do you talk about your success? Do you minimize it, so as not to seem too proud? Suggest that failure is imminent, so as not to curse the gods with your hubris? Are you making sure every time you describe something good that has resulted from your efforts to also include something you got wrong? How uncomfortable are you simply smiling and telling someone, "I did it!" (without referring to luck or someone else's role in the outcome)?

In the fall of 2013, I had a television series in development based on the book, *Happiness as a Second Language*, and a major actress came on board to play the lead. My husband and I went to a Christmas party that year at the home of a very successful TV writer. In the course of conversation with her, she asked what I was up to.

This was my reply, verbatim: "My book came out earlier this year, and now it looks like it might get made into a TV show. [Major Actress] is attached, so we'll see what happens. Of course, I haven't heard from her in weeks, so it's probably dead, but we'll see."

I didn't think twice about what I was saying, but when we got in the car to go home, my husband turned to me and asked, "Why would you do that? Why would you tell her that what you're working on is failing, especially when it's not?"

He was right. That's exactly what I had done and it's what I almost always did. It's taken a lot of self-reflection and observation, and I confess, I still get it wrong a lot, but I now make a concerted effort to present facts about myself in the sunniest light possible, without sounding overly self-aggrandizing. In other words, I shade the facts in the hue of Success.

But change is hard. In fact, it's nearly impossible if we don't understand the underlying behavior in the first place. Why do so many of us do this? What makes us want to downplay whatever greatness we may be achieving when talking to others?

Most of us were raised with the belief that it is wrong to toot your own horn. Whether it was from parents, grand-mothers, peers or teachers, at some point, each one of us had a moment when we said, "I'm really good" and someone nearby corrected us – told us not to talk that way. Our brains then formed the neural pathways that made sure whenever we were inclined to say we were good, we had to either: (a) shut up, (b) say the opposite, (c) include information about how bad we are as well, or (d) give someone or something else credit.

For me, I can trace my own uncertainty in this area to a very specific incident in junior high school. While answering a teacher's question about going to college, I said, "smart people like Brian and me..." Another girl in the room – whose name I totally remember, but will not share here – instantly howled, "Conceited," drawing out the "eeeeeedddd" forever.

For the next few weeks, whenever I walked into a room, someone would say or shout, "Conceited!"

It sent the unmistakable message that if you're smart, you cannot be the person who says it.

But what if you're a better singer?

Nope, don't say it.

A better athlete?

Um...maybe.

Prettier?

Absolutely not!

Harder working? Might be okay...or not, but only if it's true.

In polite society we have rules and taboos about self-promotion, and it feels like we walk a very fine line between being self-deprecating to the point of putting yourself down and being called conceited every time you walk into the school lunch room.

But it is not that fine a line. It's quite a broad line, we just made it narrower through our own fears of being on the wrong side of it. Talking about the innate qualities you were born with, like intelligence or good looks or a beautiful singing voice, can be distasteful, but talking about the results of your hard work or determination is fair game. Here's the simple guideline: If you've *done something* to bring about your success, you can talk about it.

It is not conceited to say, "I have a television show in development and a big star is attached," especially in response to someone asking what you're working on. There is nothing wrong with telling colleagues, "I was just put in charge of the largest account at the firm." Over lunch with a client, feel free to say, "My sales numbers are the highest they've ever been," with a huge smile on your face.

Are you at a networking function among small business owners? No one will hold it against you if you share that you just taught yourself how to build a website and it looks better than you could have ever imagined. In fact, they will probably ask for your advice. Don't dwell on how incredibly long it took you, or how much you might have gotten wrong, and if questions about that arise, give honest replies without advertising some shortcoming on your part.

Facts are facts, and you are allowed to share facts. So, where does the shading come in? You have to learn how to tell people that you are doing well *as a result of your own efforts*, without coming off as a jerk or sounding like your success is the exception, rather than the norm. State the fact of your good outcome, and when they reply, find a way to acknowledge what you did that made it happen, or talk about what you will do now that you've reached this goal.

Here are some sample conversations. When you share news of some event in your life, the other person will generally congratulate you or ask an honest question. How you reply reflects how fluent you are in your new language of Success. Always try to go with the successful reply.

Event you share: "I was just put in charge of the largest account at the firm."

Response: "Hey, congratulations!"

Self-deprecating Reply: "Well, I had the most seniority, so they had to pick me. That's all."

Jerk Reply: "Who else? I'm the only one in the department who isn't a total idiot."

Successful Reply: "Thank you. I've been working really hard to get to this point, so it's nice to see it pay off."

Event: "I have a television show in development and a big star is now attached,"

Response: "Wow! Way to go."

Self-deprecating Reply: "Actually, the actress hasn't called me in weeks, so she's probably lost interest."

Jerk Reply: "Geez, have you seen her last two movies? My show is the best thing she could do right now!"

Successful Reply: "Thanks! I'm so excited to get to the next stage. I know a lot has to fall into place to get a show on the air, but this is a great start."

Event: "My sales numbers are the highest they've ever been,"

Response: "Really?"

(No one is judging you when they ask this question, just making small talk. They might not have even heard what you just said. And even if they are judging, that's their language. You can still reply in Success.)

Self-deprecating Reply: "Of course, I'm still nowhere near the top producers and probably never will be."

Jerk Reply: "Yep! They are so lucky to have me. I could sell sand in the desert."

Successful Reply: "Yes. Once I figured out how to develop good leads and really convey the value of our product, it all came together, and I hope to build on that going forward."

Event: "I taught myself how to build a website for my business and it looks like it's going to be really effective."

Response: "How did you do that?"

Self-deprecating Reply: "It took forever! Even the simplest things tripped me up. And I know it doesn't function anywhere near as well as I need it to."

Jerk Reply: "It's not rocket science. I can't believe how much money people dumber than me get paid to do this."

Successful Reply: "There are so many resources available now, I just found a few that worked and followed their instructions. It wasn't without its challenges, but I plowed through, kept at it, and it actually looks pretty good."

Event: "My kids both made it onto the honor roll this year."

Response: "You must be so proud."

Self-deprecating Reply: "I don't know where they get it from. I was never good in school."

Jerk Reply: "Well, with me and Bob as their parents, what would you expect?"

Successful Reply: "Yes. I am. As a family, we made school a priority, so I'm happy it's working."

You'll notice that all of the self-deprecating replies have the tone of either not taking credit for your own success, attributing it to luck or someone else's actions, putting yourself down for not achieving it in the time or manner you thought it needed, or assuming it's temporary and soon it will all go away. If you really believe any of these to be true, then you need to put in some time and effort to reclaim your self-worth. You deserve the success you've worked for, and good things can come to you, so embrace and enjoy what you've built for yourself.

If, on the other hand, you are merely presenting the facts that way because you've been trained to do so, then work on breaking the habit.

And what makes the Jerk Reply so jerky? It's the suggestion that you got where you are because you are innately better than someone else. Success does not always come as a result of someone else's failure, so there's no need to put anyone else down or pump yourself up just to make an outcome sound better. In fact, it makes it sound worse.

Shading is also a great way to practice using the language of Success to get the results you desire. This is a little trickier, because you are leading the conversation, not just responding, but the principles are the same. Before talking, ask yourself what you want to convey and what you want to get out of it.

At our hypothetical Small Business Networking Event, maybe you want to make sure no one asks you to help with their website, because you don't have the time, so you shade it to convey that you're not that good at it, and hopefully they won't ask. But think about the overall result you want from the networking event. Is this really the best way to get it? Do you want people to think you are barely competent, or a time waster, or have a hard time mastering new skills? These are the messages you're sending with any reply that isn't in the language of Success.

If you're worried about being asked for help, stand firm and learn how to say, "No." Successful people do this all the time, which we will discuss at great length in Chapter Ten.

You can talk about what a good job you did with your website, and if someone asks for help with theirs, it's perfectly fine to pleasantly reply, "I couldn't help you build your site, but I'm happy to share all of the links to the resources I used. May I have your card?" If they say they are really looking for a person to handle the whole thing for them, gently and politely remind them (with a smile – smiling goes a long way), that building websites isn't your business, but someone in the room probably does that, and they should ask the organizer to make an introduction.

Think about the outcome you want – to be thought of as competent at your day-to-day work and successful in your field, and make sure all of your communication is shaded to convey that.

The final area where you can inadvertently shade your own success with failure is how you present yourself and your ideas in group settings. How many times have you been in a meeting and someone starts her comment with, "I might be wrong, but...?" Newsflash – no one wants to listen to someone who might be wrong. Discounting your own contribution is not conducive to success. Yes, you minimize personal risk by not forcefully declaring your ideas, but putting them out there without even your endorsement almost guarantees that they will be ignored.

If you're not sure how to open your contribution to a group discussion, try these:

    1. "Here's my idea..."

    2. "Let's consider this..."

    3. "What I think would work is..."

Take ownership of what you are about to say in the same way you take ownership of your success – without discounting.

In almost all corporate settings, being wrong is not considered nearly as big a flaw as being wishy-washy. Successful people are willing to be wrong. Less successful people avoid risk by being willing to abandon their own ideas at the first sign of dissent. Remember, no one will listen to you if you start out by telling them they don't have to.

EXERCISE:

Right now, think of something you've accomplished in the past three months that was entirely your own doing. You set your mind to it, you worked on it and you achieved it. Next, think of how you can describe that achievement to someone else in a way that doesn't discount what you've done, and doesn't come off as bragging. Now – the hard part. Go have that conversation! Choose three different people – maybe a friend, a co-worker and a family member; or a business affiliate, a client and the person next to you on the plane. Start with the fact of what you did, wait for their reply, then add one more sentence describing how you did it, giving yourself credit without overdoing it. The conversation should end here, unless the other person is truly interested and wants to hear more.

Congratulations! You have just spoken Success.

CHAPTER SIX

The Nouns of Success

Outcome

Judgment

A noun is a person, place, thing, quality, state of existence, concept or idea. When learning the language of Success, it is necessary to take nouns that are merely concepts, like outcome and judgment, and turn them into actual, concrete things. Doing this will make you fluent in Success.

Outcome, noun.

    1. *The way a thing turns out;*

    2. *A consequence of an action.*

If you are attempting to achieve success, you have to focus on the outcome of your actions. The actions themselves are not enough. Many say that the journey is more important than the destination, but whether that is true or not depends on your definition of success.

If you defined success as: "constantly learning and growing, without regard to any ultimate achievement," then outcomes are not as critical to your path. However, if you've defined success as reaching some pre-determined goal, like getting a corner office, being awarded tenure, selling a screenplay or taking your start-up company public, then your efforts towards that goal must be outcome-oriented.

What is the point of all the work you're doing if you take a giant left turn before reaching your goal because you stopped focusing on the outcome and instead cared more about the process? You learn and grow while getting there, but there is a "there" you must reach to be successful.

This may seem abstract, so let me share three very specific incidents where focusing on the outcome, over any other possible desires, was what led to success.

"Congratulations."

When I quit Brobeck, Phleger & Harrison in San Francisco, I chose to join Wilson Sonsini, the largest and most reputable law firm in the Silicon Valley. After interviewing extensively and accepting a very good offer, I told them I needed to take two months off before starting. I had been working 80-100 hour weeks pretty consistently for the previous year and I needed a break to get my life back in order. My new boss was going to be John Roos, an exceptional attorney and a good guy, and he agreed to postpone my start date.

During this sabbatical, I spent time helping friends who were launching start-up companies. I wrote their business plans and put together venture capital presentations, and I quickly realized that this was what I really wanted to do. I preferred to help emerging companies as a consultant rather than as a lawyer, so I decided to hang out my shingle and strike out on my own.

Now, the only thing I had to do was call John Roos and tell him. It was going to be one of the most difficult calls of my career, but I had to make it. The call went like this, word-for-word:

Valerie: "Hi, John. I have some bad news. I'm not going to be starting at Wilson Sonsini after all."
John: "Why?"
Valerie: "I've decided to start a consulting firm to help early stage companies raise venture capital."

There wasn't even a beat. Without pause, John said one word that will forever be etched in my mind as one of the greatest lessons in business, politics and diplomacy I've ever learned.

He said: "Congratulations."

I breathed an enormous sigh of relief and said, "Thank you."

We quickly got off the phone, since he immediately had to begin the process of finding and recruiting my replacement (at a time when there was a severe scarcity of experienced corporate securities lawyers in the area), but he never let me know that. He was focused enough on the outcome to know that no good would come of losing his temper, or telling me what a disservice I was doing to his practice, and for that, I showed my gratitude by sending him every single company I worked with that needed legal representation. I will never know how John truly felt about the choice I made, although I can't imagine he was happy about it, but I will always know how to respond when someone lets me down in a way that could work out in my favor in the long run – as long as I stay focused on the outcome.

One Evaluation, Two Very Different Outcomes

I joined the small boutique investment bank, SG Cowen, as a corporate finance associate to help re-launch their Internet banking practice in 1998. Another associate (we'll call him "Stan") was brought into the corporate finance group from the private equity department at the same time, and we were supposed to be the "Internet bankers." Only there was one problem – for the first few months we were there, SG Cowen didn't have a research analyst in the Internet space.

Without going into detail, I will say that it is nearly impossible for an investment bank to get a client's corporate finance business if they don't have an analyst to cover the stock. Stan and I had very little to do, other than try and drum up business or build pitch books for other bankers' meetings.

This fact did not make for a good performance review. What also did not make for a good performance review was the fact that SG Cowen had only recently been acquired by the French bank, Société Générale, whose American head-quarters were in New York. My boss, the head of technology banking, had scarcely spent any time with his boss, the new CEO, when the CEO called one morning and said, "I'll be in town tomorrow for employee evaluations, so get those ready today and clear your schedule." To put it bluntly, not a lot of time and thought was put into these reviews.

Stan and I were office mates, and he got called to the conference room first. I had no delusions about how a review might go for a banker who hadn't worked on a deal since being hired, but perhaps Stan did. Everything they said to him about his work, he threw back at them about theirs. Of course he wasn't working on any deals, but that was because they weren't bringing any in. Yes, he had to spend time on business development (a no-no for associates at our level), since clearly no one above him was doing any. According to him, his analytical skills were not lacking in any way, which is what they were saying, they just weren't being utilized because there was *nothing to do*!

It went on and on. Another associate whose office was next to the conference room came down the hall and poked her head into my office to see if there was anything I could do to get Stan out of there. She'd never heard so much screaming. Finally, he stormed back in, slamming his coat into his chair and ranting about these idiots who have no idea how to run their own bank. As he paced and fumed, my phone rang. I looked at the call screen. It said, "Conference Room." *Great.*

As I walked down the hall, I reminded myself that there was one outcome I wanted – I needed – from this meeting, and I had to stay focused on getting that. No matter what they said, stay focused on the outcome.

Here is a transcript of what happened in my review, which I wrote down as soon as I got back to my office that day and have kept all these years. At the time, I thought I might need it for some potential unlawful termination case (always thinking like a lawyer...), but I guess the universe just wanted me to have it for this book. What good fortune!

I walked in, sat down, exchanged greetings with the men, and then it started.

CEO: "So we have to get to your review, and I can tell you it's not good."

He then turned to my boss and indicated that he should start the critique.

Boss: "You don't have anywhere near the workload that your colleagues are handling, and it doesn't look so hot."

Valerie: "I agree. It's been so disappointing. As you know, I was an IPO lawyer before this, so until we have Internet deals in the pipeline, I'd be happy to hop onto any other team and help out as needed. Would that be allowed?"

They look at each other, shrug and agree it should be, so I continue: "That's great. If you could keep your ears open for any opportunities like that and let me know, I'd appreciate it. And I'm happy to work out of the New York office, if that's needed."

They agree. In fact, they think this is a pretty good idea. Then my boss moves down the page.

Boss: "You spend far too much time on business development, which we can't have associates doing."

Valerie: "No problem. I didn't realize that, but I'll stop."

Again, they are taken aback by my agreement.

Boss: "Good. Also, you seem to lack the analytical skills you need to perform this job."

(Side note here – I have a Masters degree in economics from Berkeley. I scored one point shy of a perfect score on the Law School Admissions Test – 1/3 of which consists of analytical games. I lack many skills in life, but the very basic numerical analysis required for corporate finance is not among them. My boss thought I lacked analytical skills because I had not worked on any deals that might require them because he and his cohort hadn't brought in any business. No wonder Stan spent half an hour screaming at them!)

Unlike Stan, I bit my tongue. In this meeting, I am focused on an outcome – one key outcome – so I reply: "I wasn't aware of that. Are there any courses I should be looking at, or just some books I can try to work through?" The men are now completely stymied. The CEO leaps in.

CEO: "I think it's just something you will develop over time."

Valerie: "Okay. Good."

I can see there are four more points on my written evaluation to go over, but both men look at each other and it's clear that they aren't really interested in continuing with this. I can also see Stan's evaluation on the table next to mine. The two documents are identical. He and I were given the exact same evaluation.

CEO: "So, do you have any questions for us?"

Valerie: "There is one thing. When I was hired, I agreed to come in as a first-year associate for the purpose of my advancement track, but given my years practicing law, I was supposed to be paid as a third-year associate, which hasn't happened."

CEO: "I think we can take care of that."

Valerie: "Thank you. Will that be retroactive to my start date?"

CEO: "Yes. It should be. Is there anything else?"

Valerie: "No. I will work on improving in all the areas we discussed."

They both thanked me and I left.

That Friday, Stan got fired, and I got a check for $10,000.

No matter how painful the process is getting there, always stay focused on the outcome.

"Get Them to Help You Get a Better Job"

A friend of mine has worked at a large university for the past seven years. In that time, the culture has changed quite a bit and she has become increasingly angered by its policies. At the same time, her daughter will be starting school next fall and she wants a job that starts later in the day, with a less taxing commute, so that she can spend time with her daughter in the morning and drive her to school every day.

When we talked about her quitting next year, she was very concerned that she might have to take a year or two to find the perfect situation, since she would probably be parting on bad terms. In the meantime, she is having more and more conflicts at work as she tries to get the school to develop more favorable policies.

With all that in mind, I told her to step back and focus on the outcome. In the military, the phrase for someone in their last three months of active duty is "short-timer." A soldier or an officer will refer to a colleague as having "short-timer's disease," which means they have checked out and stopped caring.

I reminded my friend that, for all intents and purposes, she is a short-timer. Why should she care what the vacation and sick-leave policy is if she will be quitting before it ever affects her? I know she is trying to get the university to do the right thing for everyone else, but that doesn't help her reach her desired outcome, which is to get a better job. All it does is put her in the line of fire at a time when she needs her superiors to be her strongest allies.

She has a perfect reason for why she needs to find another job, so there should be no hard feelings about her leaving, and she will stay through the end of the academic year, so she will not be leaving them in a lurch. All she has to do now is work on being as pleasant and easy to work with as possible, so that when she does go, they'll regret losing her.

What they will also do is say nice things about her to anyone who asks. My advice for her was to put signs up where she can easily see them (yes, actual physical signs), for whenever she is tempted to leap into some conflict or controversy. The signs should read: "What is my goal?" No need to write the answer (for anyone else to see), but every time she looks at it, it will remind her to stay focused on the outcome.

Her goal is to get her current employers to help her land a better job. Her goal is *not* to force them into enacting policies for the benefit of the remaining workforce after she's gone. Her goal is not even to complete some major task or project before she goes, to have some esoteric sense of accomplishment. Her goal is simply to do whatever it takes to make them miss her when she's gone.

Fighting with her employers right up until the day she turns in her keys and ID will not make any difference in how they behave the day after she's gone, and will only make them think less of her. It will be so challenging to remain silent in the face of issues she has confronted in the past, but as long as she is focused on the outcome – the better job with more freedom and flexibility for her as a parent – she will make the right choices.

The best way to get to the outcome you want is to write it down, and make sure not only that you are actively working to achieve it, but that none of your actions work against it. If you are tempted to speak up to start a conflict, or even to tell your boss what she's doing wrong in her job, stop and ask if that gets you closer to your desired outcome. Unless you suffer from a mental illness, you have control over what comes out of your mouth, so keep your goals in mind before you decide to leap into a fight or share a story that may not be appropriate for the workplace.

If the outcome you want is to get next Friday off, then it's not a good idea to criticize your manager's tie, no matter how ugly it is. Often in the workplace, if it feels good saying it, maybe it shouldn't be said.

Staying focused on the outcome is one of the hallmarks of a native speaker of Success.

Now, you may be thinking, "How is it success if I have to become a self-centered, result-oriented jackass to get there?"

Again, this depends both on your definition of success and your honest assessment of the outcomes you can achieve. In my investment banking example, my definition of success was to keep the job and get paid the salary I signed on for. None of that required telling my boss everything he was doing wrong, particularly in front of his boss. Even if my goal was to build and expand the Internet banking practice, the only way to do so was to keep my job and make sure my boss saw me as a team player, willing to learn and grow.

My behavior during the performance review, although singularly focused on getting more money, also had the tangential benefit of making me someone that both my boss and the CEO were willing to listen to as my work there continued, which in the long run may have led to a stronger Internet banking practice. We'll never know because a few months after the terrible review, I got a great job offer to be an executive at an Internet start-up, an outcome I could have never predicted, but which only happened because I didn't get fired that day.

If you find yourself conflicted because you want to leave a company whose policies are having a negative effect on the entire workforce, but you feel it's selfish to just stay positive and keep the boss happy until you find a better job, then here is where an honest assessment is required. Truthfully – how much of a difference can you really make in your limited time there?

Brutal self-awareness can be painful in this situation, but the truth is, if you are not in a position to set policy, and your only contribution to any potential improvement is to continuously make your employer aware that there are problems, you will not effect any real change. You will only serve to alienate the people whose endorsements you need to move on to your next opportunity, while at the same time not improving the workplace for anyone else. That is not success by anyone's definition.

Also, staying positive in a negative environment – even if you are doing so for personal, success-driven reasons – makes the workplace better for everyone around you. That, in turn, makes you someone who others will want to work with again and again, which is an amazing outcome to achieve in any quest for success.

EXERCISE:

IN ONE INTERACTION TODAY where you feel challenged or are unsure how to proceed, stop and ask yourself, "What is my desired outcome?" Re-focus your behavior and efforts solely on achieving that desired outcome. Block out any other needs or wants, like getting others to say you're right, or making sure some additional thing is taken care of right now. With singular focus, pursue your desired outcome.

Judgment, noun.

1. *an opinion or decision based on careful thought;*

2. *the process of forming an opinion after careful thought;*

3. *the ability to make good decisions;*

4. *the opinion of others towards something or someone.*

In the language of Success, Judgment is an irregular noun. There are parts of the definition that you need to practice and embrace and parts that you need to reject.

The first three definitions of the word Judgment are very useful in your drive towards success. If you are inclined to make hasty choices or rash decisions, force yourself to apply careful thought before reaching a conclusion. Slow yourself down, and even take a moment to write the pros and cons of your options down, review them carefully, then come to a conclusion. It may be the exact same conclusion that you started with, and that's fine, as long as you have solid reasoning for how you got there.

Do this more and more, and you will gain greater confidence in your own judgment, and become better able to defend it in the face of challenges. As you grow and gain experience, not only will you learn to trust your judgment, but others will as well, which may be critical for your success.

That said, how others judge you should not be a primary consideration when determining a course of action, which is why the definition of Judgment that you must jettison is the fourth one: "the opinion of others towards something or someone."

The world is full of people just eager and waiting to pass judgment on your choices, your definition of success, the path you've chosen to get there, the dream you've decided to pursue and whatever else crosses their minds. You cannot let this affect your decisions.

In the next chapter, we'll learn that the most important action verb in the language of Success is Decide. Sometimes, in order to decide, you have to block out the negative forces that want to tell you there's no chance, or worse, that you're not the right person to do it. Sometimes, the decision you have to make is going to invite the exact judgments you are trying to avoid. It doesn't matter. If it's the right choice, you have to make it, no matter what others will say.

The most dreaded judgments from others occur when you realize that the journey you've been on will not lead to the success you desire, and to be successful, you must change direction. We cripple ourselves with the fear of letting the world know and what their reactions may be, but that is the exact time when we are making the bravest, most success-oriented choices, and it is imperative to keep that in mind.

As discussed in Chapter Four, changing direction is not failure, no matter what anyone else wants to call it. Sticking with something that you know is not the right fit, sacrificing a potentially better path because it is not the well-trod one, or preventing yourself from giving 100% to your dreams because you are concerned about what others will say or think is a far greater failure than deciding to stop one pursuit and move on to the next one. Be brave and do what you must to reach your goals, even if those goals have changed, even if someone in your sphere feels the need to mock that choice.

Anyone can sit back and pass judgment. It is the easiest action a person can take, and many make it their primary pastime. If you are among these people, stop it. You aren't making the world a better place by rolling your eyes, giggling at someone else's attempts, announcing that you think someone's goal or journey is a waste. Worse, you are hampering your own efforts. What you put out into the atmosphere is what will come back to you. Support others in their dreams and you should get their support in return, but even if you don't, it's still the right thing to do.

The harder act than not passing judgment is to ignore the judgment of others as you strive towards success. In fact, fear of this judgment can be so powerful that you may make decisions based on it even when it's not present. In other words, you are so convinced that others will judge you that you alter your course before they even have the chance. This can be disastrous.

The newspaper columnist, Judith Martin, a.k.a. Miss Manners, wrote the greatest line I've ever read on this topic. She said, "People would not worry so much about what others thought of them if they realized how seldom they did." That is to say, with the possible exception of your immediate family, the rest of the population is not spending their days concerned with whether or not you are on a frivolous journey.

At most, they might have a fleeting thought, make a snarky comment, post a smug remark about you online, and that will be all. You can survive that!

Another person's negative response is rarely about your efforts and almost always about their own fears and failures, so when you are in the presence of a person who is radiating negativity towards your success, picture the green, gaseous cloud that must be enveloping them. Picture them in the center of a pool of noxious smoke, choking out the support you should be getting. Then, it becomes less about the person and more about that part of them that has to behave this way.

You can maintain the relationship, without bitterness or resentment, when you separate the person from the negative energy. Breathe easy knowing that a cloud like that is not emanating from you. Hear their words, and respond if you so choose, but do not let their doubts and judgments sink in. Leave it trapped in that green cloud. This is a very effective technique for dealing with highly toxic people.

Another technique for dealing with a milder form of judgment – unwanted advice, pestering questions, not-so-subtle suggestions of a different path (like the mother who brings you a job application the week after you start your graphic design business) – is to erect imaginary shields between you and the other person.

These people are not toxic, but their energy is not conducive to your progress. Next time you are faced with someone questioning the value of your goals or your ability to reach them, silently say to yourself, "Energy shields UP!" then picture an invisible, unbreakable wall forming between the two of you.

You can still hear their words, but their negativity will bounce right off the wall, back at them. You don't absorb, you don't flare up, and you don't let your motivation get hampered. You can respond, calm and cool, because you are not taking on their doubts about you. I like to pretend this wall is a solid sheet of ice, and picture the other person's words slamming into it and sliding down to a puddle.

As a bonus, this technique works in dealing with all sorts of toxic people in the workplace – the bully, the gossip, the complainer, the person whose energy just sucks yours up. If the outcome you desire requires you to deal with a person who pollutes the air with their attitude or behavior, stay focused on your success by keeping these shields up.

These visualization techniques can get you a long way towards preventing the judgment of others from interfering with your success. However, you still have to be careful not to allow the fear of it to creep into your decision-making.

The worst time I ever succumbed to the judgment of others involved judgment that existed solely in my own mind. I have never revealed this to anyone prior to writing it here, but it's time to come clean.

In the year 2000, when I was leaving San Francisco to move back to Indiana to help my mother recover from brain surgery, I knew the departure was permanent. I had a huge going-away party, full of friends, former clients, co-workers and neighbors, and I told everyone that I would be back in a year, but I knew that wasn't true. I knew that after Indiana, I would be moving to Hollywood to become a screenwriter.

I didn't tell a single person. I thought they would laugh at me.

Worse, because I was so convinced that I had to keep up the charade that I'd be coming back there, I put my remaining belongings in a local storage unit, and did not even consider looking at housing in Los Angeles before leaving.

Given the circumstances, I wish I'd just been honest with everyone. I wish I had taken the profit I'd earned from the sale of my house and bought a home in Los Angeles, an area whose real estate market had not yet come close to the surge that the San Francisco market was experiencing at the time, and rented it out while I was away. That would have provided some income while I spent time in Indiana with my mom, and given me a place to land upon my return to California. I also wish I'd hired movers to take my things south immediately, and put them in storage there.

All of this may seem like afterthoughts, but the truth is, these are all things I thought of doing at the time, and the only reason I didn't – *the only reason* – was that I didn't want to tell anyone what my plan was, because I thought they might judge me.

Now, I am the first person to say that everything happens exactly as it's supposed to, and when I did arrive in LA, I met with unexpected success breaking into the entertainment business, in part because of neighbors who worked in the industry and provided access and advice. Perhaps that would not have materialized if I owned a place in another part of town, but I will never know. I do know that I made an unwise financial decision about how to pursue my goals, even after deciding to pursue them, simply to dodge judgment, which is very foolish.

An added risk of allowing the judgment of others to affect your behavior and impede your success is that, in an effort to appear cooperative, you may wind up negotiating against yourself. You don't want them to think badly of you, or see you as greedy or grabby, so you lead by asking for less than you should. This is a mistake. Don't start your negotiations by giving the other side an advantage over you.

Do not approach transactions with the other party's opinion of you in mind over your own needs, goals and outcomes. Let the other side take care of themselves as regards what they think of you and what they ask for. If your first move is to offer concessions or take perks off the table for yourself, or if your initial dollar amount is the exact amount you're looking for, you have nowhere to go but down. Asking for what you're worth does not make you greedy. It makes you strong and it's what successful people do.

One of my most visceral memories is of a comment made to me by my real estate agent when I was selling my house in the Bay Area. The market was very hot and the highest bidders (who did not know they were the highest), included an impassioned letter with their offer about how much they wanted the house, so upon reviewing all of the offers, I told my agent to counter them on price. She was shocked. Their bid was substantially more than the next one, but I thought they would go higher. She said to me, "It's your karma," as if I was doing something wrong.

I said nothing about this comment at the time, and I regret that. Months after the transaction was closed, when I found out she committed fraud to get those buyers to drop out so that friends of hers could buy the house for $17,000 less, I made the choice to just walk away and chalk it up as a lesson in following my instincts. Her judgment of me didn't make me back down from my position, but when she made the comment about my karma, I should have known not to trust her to represent my interests, and should have been more vigilant for the rest of that transaction. I also should have realized that she was the one worried about karma.

Do not let anyone else's opinion of your success, or pursuit thereof, cloud your good judgment. Create a barrier between their negative energy and your success-fueled objectives, and move ahead with your actions. If you decide to change direction after working towards a particular goal, tune out those who find that amusing, or just want to make it a topic of catty conversation. Staying on the wrong path is a far greater failure than switching to a different one.

And if you're worried about people judging you behind your back, remember, they're behind you for a reason.

BONUS NOUN

Integrity, noun

1. *The quality of being honest*

2. *Having strong moral values*

3. *Internal consistency or lack of corruption*

Integrity is one of those nouns that has an enormous value over the course of a career, and yet, there are numerous examples of people we see as successful who operate entirely without it. That's why this is the bonus section – because this noun is not *mandatory* for success, but I'd strongly encourage embracing it.

Once you possess true integrity, and everyone you deal with knows it, finding allies in your pursuit of success becomes much easier. The road may still be rough, especially as you encounter those who lack integrity, but your foundation will be more solid, and you will bounce back from adversity more quickly and smoothly.

In the movie, *Jerry Maguire*, Jerry, a sports agent, reaches an agreement with the father of a football player he wants to represent, then tries to get him to sign a contract, to which the man replies, "My word is my bond."

A bond is what you put up in promise of some future performance. When someone is arrested, they're set free by paying a bond as a promise that they will appear in court. Insurance companies will bond a movie, to promise the investors that they will get their money back in the event the movie cannot be completed.

When you use a phrase like, "My word is my bond," you are telling the other person that your word – your commitment, your vow, your spoken promise – is as good as a signed piece of paper or a good-faith payment of money. If you say that, it has to be true every time. *Every single time.* If it's not true even once, you will have destroyed whatever reputation you have built over the course of your career, and it will be almost impossible to get back to the point where someone can rely on your word.

Depending on your personal definition of success, integrity may or may not be required, and everyone's interpretation of what it means to have integrity may be different. In my own dealings, I strive to always behave with integrity, and I expect it of those I work with. I will forgive all kinds of incompetence, errors in judgment, failures to perform and so on, but if someone shows a lack of integrity, I do everything in my power not to work with them again, and if I have to, it is only with extreme caution.

On a business note, no matter how strong someone's word is, when you reach an agreement with another party, put it in writing. Every time. Make sure both parties understand, agree to and are clear on all of the terms, and if the other side refuses to sign it, then you do not have an agreement. Period. If you think for a moment that you will be fine, even without a signed document, go watch the movie *Jerry Maguire*.

CHAPTER SEVEN

THE PRIMARY VERB OF SUCCESS

Decide

"When I said that nothing had been done I erred in one important matter. We had definitely committed ourselves and were halfway out of our ruts. This may sound too simple, but it is great in consequence. Until one is committed, there is hesitancy, the chance to draw back, always ineffectiveness. Concerning all acts of initiative (and creation), there is one elementary truth, the ignorance of which kills countless ideas and splendid plans: that the moment one definitely commits oneself, the providence moves too. A whole stream of events issues from the decision, raising in one's favor all manner of unforeseen incidents, meetings and material assistance, which no man could have dreamt would have come his way. I learned a deep respect for one of Goethe's couplets: Whatever you can do or dream you can, begin it. Boldness has genius, power and magic in it!"

— W. H. Murray, *The Scottish Himalaya Expedition*

Verbs are actions, and the most powerful action you can take in the pursuit of any endeavor is to decide to do it. Until you decide, there can be no forward momentum. Deciding is how you launch everything else. As the rock band Rush says in the song, *Freewill*: "If you choose not to decide, you still have made a choice." In the language of Success, the phrase, "I choose not to decide" translates into: "I choose to fail."

In 2005, a friend and I wrote a short film and decided to make it. Neither of us had ever been involved in anything like this before – we had never even worked on anyone else's independent production. I had never directed a film, and yet, I decided to direct. We had never produced a film, and yet, we decided to produce this one.

It was crazy, and there is no reason we should have succeeded, but we did. Our vision made it onto the screen, simply because we decided that it would.

We actually never questioned that we would be able to do this, and that is probably why it happened. Maybe ignorance is bliss, but the idea of plowing headlong into a goal, not knowing that you have no business achieving that goal, can move mountains in ways you might not have imagined possible. We looked at what was needed to make a movie, broke the big steps down into small, achievable goals, and worked towards them daily.

Our little film came out okay, not great, but I am still exceedingly proud of it. Why? Because it made it to a screen, which is how I defined success for this project. It was the first thing I ever produced or directed. It had a 39-member crew, 26 speaking roles, 7 extras, and a large post-production team, all working tirelessly for this to become a reality. What could possibly be unsuccessful about that?

Decide, and quite possibly, like Mr. Murray above on his expedition to Mt. Everest, a whole stream of events will issue from the decision, raising in your favor all manner of unforeseen incidents, meetings and material assistance, which you could not have dreamt would happen.

This chapter opens with the Murray quote for two reasons. The first is that it introduces the concept of luck (or divine intervention, which he refers to as providence) following the decision. While there is no scientific proof of this, I have found in my life that when I made an unwavering decision to pursue something, the luck always followed, and when I was working towards something that seemed less favored by the universe, in hindsight, I had to admit that I had not really committed to it fully in the first place.

This is not a form of "sour grapes" (from the fable where the fox can't reach the grapes on the branch above him, so decides they must have been sour anyway). It is the result of honest self-examination. After not achieving success in something, I reflect on what went wrong, and almost every time, realize that I was never really certain of the goal to start with.

By no means am I saying that people who experience bad luck pursuing success don't really want it badly enough. Bad fortune happens to all sorts of people — good, nasty, deserving, committed — and that may have nothing to do with how decisively they are pursuing their goals. I have always found it insulting when someone explains a sports team's victory with the phrase, "They just wanted it more." It can't be true that every defeated team in history simply did not want to win as much as their opponent.

What I am saying is that making a clear decision makes the path much easier. If you want to make a film, decide to make it. If you want to start a company, decide to start it. If you want to be a rock star, decide to be one.

Louis Pasteur said, "Chance favors the prepared mind." In other words, prepare for success, and allow the luck to happen. Preparing starts with making the decision as the first action, the first verb, then following with the actions in Chapter Four (setting your monthly goals and daily tasks), which are made easier once you are committed. "Luck" or "providence" or "the universe" will then do its part. Your journey will not be without its setbacks, but be open to seeing and taking advantage of the fortune that comes from deciding. It will be there.

The second reason I included the passage above about the Himalayan Expedition is that it contains a quote attributed to Goethe, which I want to discuss further when it comes to your success.

"What you can do, or dream you can do, begin it; Boldness has genius, power and magic in it."

I remember the first time I ever saw those words. It was my freshman year of college and they popped up on half a dozen dorm room doors. I'd never seen the quote before, and frankly, it didn't do anything for me. I didn't equate starting a new task with "boldness" and didn't understand why it was so special.

It was only years later, when I came across the full passage from John Anster's loose translation of Goethe's play, *Faust*, that this couplet really spoke to me.

The full quote reads:
> *Indecision brings its own delays,*
> *And days are lost lamenting over lost days.*
> *Are you in earnest?*
> *Seize this very minute;*
> *What you can do, or dream you can, begin it;*
> *Boldness has genius, power and magic in it.*

"Indecision brings its own delays."

I cannot count how many things in life I've missed out on because I simply couldn't make the decision to do them. Quick, confident decision-making has been an important survival skill for humans for two million years, since first discovering that if you threw the spear at just the right moment, the wooly mammoth died and the tribe ate.

However, we now have far more factors that go into our decisions than our cave-dwelling ancestors, and we can get overwhelmed with our ability to second-guess ourselves. No one should proceed entirely without caution, but you also must reach the point where if you want a thing, you decide to go for it. Don't let indecision be the cause of any further delays.

"And days are lost lamenting over lost days."

If you didn't decide yesterday, then decide today. Don't lose today wondering whether you should have decided yesterday. As one of my close friends says, "Don't *should* all over yourself."

Think back at how many days you may have lost lamenting over lost days. Not just in your career, but in personal relationships, missed educational opportunities, heartbreaks or financial setbacks. This is a serious impediment to success. I know how hard it is to let go of regrets over past decisions, but think of those regrets as roadblocks that are keeping you from making the decisions you need to make now.

Every day spent lamenting a lost day becomes another lamentable lost day, but more importantly, it becomes another day that could have been spent getting closer to your dreams. Helen Keller, a woman who overcame more than most of us could ever imagine, had the perfect explanation for this, in terms of thrown-away opportunities to be happy. She said, "When one door of happiness closes, another opens; but often we look so long at the closed door that we do not see the one which has been opened for us." Now, replace the word "happiness" with "success" and you'll see what you miss by lamenting lost days. If you are struggling with this, don't worry, in Chapter Eleven there's a great exercise for learning how to annihilate your regret.

"Are you in earnest? Seize this very minute."

It is worth it to take a step back and answer the first question before proceeding: "Are you in earnest?" Is this really what you want? Are you able to proceed in the face of doubt, uncertainty or the outright ridicule of others? Only if you are sure of your goal can you decide to pursue it and reap the benefits (and luck) that result from making that decision.

For years, I volunteered with an organization that had a very competent and dedicated assistant, until one day I went in and found out she was on a leave of absence. At

40, she had taken time from work to travel to Texas, train, and try out for the Dallas Cowboy Cheerleaders. This was not a ridiculous pipe dream. She had been a dancer and a cheerleader for a professional sports team throughout her 20s, and always regarded the Dallas squad as the ultimate achievement. So she went for it.

I remember those in and around the organization who smirked, shared smug looks, or outright made disparaging comments about this pursuit, but I found it so courageous and admirable. It is such a better choice to give it a shot than live with the regret of never trying, never knowing!

She did not make the squad, but what she gained was the knowledge that she would not have, which is a form of success in itself. In earnest, she seized the moment, put forth her best efforts to pursue a lifelong dream, and discovered that it was not an option for her any more, so she could now happily and confidently change direction. Remember — changing direction is not failure.

Now, she will never have to live with the lingering uncertainty of not having tried. I was so proud of and happy for her. What a waste it would have been if she'd never decided to try. She seized the very minute, so no more days could be lost lamenting over lost days.

"What you can do, or dream you can, begin it."

Beginning it is the result of making the decision. The way to begin to pursue success is to decide to pursue success. If you dream that you can do it, then begin it, because…

"Boldness has genius, power and magic in it."

Going back to the W.H. Murray passage that opened this chapter — once you decide, a whole stream of events issues from the decision, raising all manner of unforeseen incidents, meetings and material assistance, which no person could have dreamt would come their way. That's the genius, power and magic that you will experience and enjoy.

You are reading this book because you seek success in some field or endeavor. In Chapter Two, you defined success for yourself in that pursuit. In Chapter Three you learned how to count your accomplishments each day. In Chapter Four, you made a calendar of monthly goals and daily tasks. In Chapter Five, you started talking to others about your achievements with the shading of success. In Chapter Six you focused on your desired outcomes and eschewed the judgments of others.

Now you have one more step to take.

Chapter Seven Exercise: Decide.

CHAPTER EIGHT

THE ACTION VERBS OF SUCCESS

Engage
Capitalize
Reward
Compare

As we covered in the previous chapter, the most important verb of Success is Decide. You cannot make any progress without deciding on a goal and making a commitment to that decision. However, once you decide to move forward towards success, as you've defined it for yourself, there are three important verbs that will move you towards your final, successful outcome: Engage, Capitalize and Reward, and one that could move you dangerously away from it: Compare.

Engage, verb

1. *occupy*
2. *attract*
3. *involve*
4. *participate in*

Nearly every business school, book, guru and blog will have some lesson or another about networking. Network, network, network! They'll tell you to use it as a verb, as you network throughout your industry, and as a noun as you build your personal network.

If you take nothing else from this book (and I hope that's not the case...), then please at least do this – lose the word "network" from your vocabulary. Nobody wants to feel networked. People are not computers. People want to feel engaged. They want to feel that you are truly interested in what they have to say and offer, and that you have something to offer that can capture their imaginations and generate excitement.

Don't think of anyone in your life as a piece of a network, no matter what role they fill or in what capacity you know them. Think of them individually as friends, colleagues, acquaintances, co-workers or mentors, realizing that some will fit into more than one category, and that's beneficial. People will be far more attracted to you if they don't sense a goal-driven mercenary trying to maximize the value of the connection, but rather a fellow human being with whom they want to have an ongoing relationship.

When you walk into a business event, don't think of "networking" the room, think of finding individuals and engaging with them. Be as interested in what they have to say as you are in talking about what you have to offer. When you discover that someone is not of great interest to your immediate efforts, find out what they need and see if you can provide it to them. This is how to build lasting alliances, which may never be of any tangible benefit to you, but more likely might. If you quickly assess that there are other people you need to meet, and you have a limited time, it's okay to say to the person in front of you, "It was so nice meeting you. Do you have a card?" Then, once you get their card and give them yours, or just trade information from phone to phone, say, "Thank you," and move away, leaving them with the feeling of having made a real connection.

Making connections can be challenging, but it's much easier when your goal is to engage the other person, not simply to make them aware of your presence.

One of my sidelines in the entertainment industry is moderating Q&A sessions with writers, directors and stars during what is known as Awards Season. When a "prestige" movie comes out, the studio or distributor will launch a campaign to win awards, which generally includes screening the movie for industry audiences and having the talent involved show up for question-and-answer sessions afterwards. At the end of these Q&As, a small percentage of the audience will usually come up to the talent to talk to them personally, which means that part of my task as the host is to stick nearby, just to make sure nobody's time is monopolized and no lines of propriety are crossed.

As a result, I've spent hours upon hours standing next to major celebrities, observing how total strangers talk to them. Almost without exception, everyone who decides to approach a star comes up and starts talking about themselves – where they're from, what they do, how much their life might be like that of some character in a movie. Only rarely have I ever seen an audience member ask the star anything about the star's life, or even about their work, and if they do, it is often just a pretext to then start talking about what the audience member really wants to talk about – themselves.

My favorite example of this was when I moderated a Q&A with a director who was dating the actress Heather Graham at the time. Heather came to the Q&A, and she and I stood off to the side as her boyfriend, the director, was mobbed by the crowd, but one woman broke off to come talk to her. The woman walked up and enthusiastically said, "HI!" Heather, who could not have been sweeter or more friendly, replied, "Hi." The woman stood there, staring at her for an uncomfortable 3-4 seconds, then said, "My name's Heather, too!"

I get it – whether encountering a movie star or walking into a room of potential business connections, it's hard to know what to say, but it is much easier if you think, *"How can I engage with this person? How can I occupy, attract and involve them?"* Think of a good question to open with. Are you at a conference together? Try, "What was the most informative session you've been in so far?" Is it a networking event for a particular industry? A good one is, "How long have you worked in this field?"

Part two of this technique is to listen to the other person's answer. That means actually *listen!* Do not just wait for them to stop talking so you can hop in with what you want to say, or hang onto their words until they say something that you might be able to talk about. Listening is a skill, and I strongly encourage you to perfect it. In each encounter, decide in advance that you will sacrifice talking about yourself until asked, and if you're never asked, then that is another way to measure the value of that connection. In all human interactions – business or otherwise – knowledge has value, and you will gain a lot more knowledge listening than talking.

Still, it can be hard to engage with total strangers. When needed, I have a go-to ice breaker that I learned while volunteering in a writing program for ten year-olds. To learn everyone's names quickly, we asked each participant, volunteer and student alike, to say their name, then tell a story about their name. It turns out that even at ten, everyone has at least one story about their name. So, when meeting someone new, if there seems to be no common topic of conversation, I will sometimes say, "When I first meet people, I always want to hear the story of their name. It seems everyone's name has a story. Do you have one?"

Sometimes it's as simple as which relative they were named for, which often leads to interesting conversations about culture and heritage, and once, a woman replied, "My name is Jane, it has no story." So I asked, "Really, your parents had no reason to pick that name?" To which she replied, "By the time I was born, my mother was so sick of having children that she refused to name me after anyone in the family and she just announced, 'I'm naming her Jane. That's it.' because it was the plainest name she could think of."

So the reality was, her name did have a story, one in which I was able to learn a lot about her, and after that we had a wonderful conversation about older siblings, parenting styles and all kinds of emotional needs she might have had as a result of her mother's attitude, which was great for both of us, me being a Happiness coach and all.

When you approach any new person or situation in your pursuit of success, work on being fully engaged. Be present in the moment, and actively listen to what the other person has to say.

And this should go without saying, but engaged people aren't looking at their phones. Unless you are a heart surgeon and someone is dying on the table, I'd be willing to bet you can get through a five minute conversation without having to check your phone. If it rings, or a text comes in, let it go, finish what you're discussing, then excuse yourself and go see what is needed. Whatever is happening on the other end of that phone is likely to be less important than the impression you're leaving on the person speaking with you if you take the call or reply to the text.

If you are not engaged, fully and at the exclusion of lesser distractions, how will you pick up on it when the CEO you just met casually mentions needing someone to do the kind of work you specialize in? Which financier will toss your card in the trash bin because you never asked a single question about her unique investment philosophy? What opportunities to learn from the mistakes of someone who runs a business in your exact field will you miss? How do you expect to catch that shooting star whose tail might just take you to the sky if you are completely focused on getting to make your point? Engage, and you will get all of those things right, and more.

Capitalize, verb

1. *to utilize an opportunity to gain an advantage*
2. *to secure funding for a venture*

There are countless business books to guide you through the second definition above in terms of calculating how much money you need to start a new venture and various ways to raise it. That will not be discussed here. Instead, in the language of Success, we focus only on the verb Capitalize as it relates to seizing a situation and using it to your maximum advantage.

If you were not raised in a household or community where success was commonly pursued and achieved, you might be hesitant to aggressively pursue an opportunity, either because you feel social constraints or have some insecurity about your offering. Shed these self-limiters, and when you see a chance to move forward, take it.

I had the privilege of attending Trinity University, a small, private college in Texas where a lot of very wealthy people send their children. I was there on scholarship. Having come from a small town in Indiana where I don't remember anyone being that rich (or that poor), this was my first full view of real money, and real income disparity, and it intimidated me. A lot.

There were people in my class who had buildings on campus named after their families. One student's last name was the same as the city he was from, which was not just some grand coincidence, and other last names were recognizable from the products and appliances that were used in my home growing up or the companies that I heard about on the news. One of my freshman classmates totaled the new Jaguar that she'd gotten for her high school graduation and a week later, a flatbed truck rolled onto campus delivering her new one. Yes, that really happened.

The first week of school, a fellow freshman came into the laundry room one night and said she didn't know how to do laundry, so I showed her. When I asked who did the laundry in her house, she shrugged and said, "One of the maids." I instantly decided that I didn't like her, based solely on that interaction, which I realize in hindsight was a defense mechanism. What I was really deciding was that she wouldn't like me, since my family never had a single maid, much less "maids," so I rejected her first. It was the start of a pattern – avoid the rich kids, stick with the scholarship students, only make friends with people who are just like me.

It was one of the biggest mistakes of my life. College is the best time to grow and form new, lasting connections, and instead of capitalizing on that opportunity, I stayed within my comfort zone, mostly out of fear. As a result, now, twenty years later, there are people from my school who I would love to be able to pick up the phone and ask advice from or do business with who I have no personal connection to. One of the most success-oriented things you can do is engage with people of all income levels, all races, all nationalities and all backgrounds. You never know who might turn out to be your closest friend.

And that woman from the laundry room freshman year? She joined the soccer team the following year, which I was on, and I found out that her mother had died when she was 16, which is probably why no one ever showed her how to do laundry. What a missed opportunity to truly engage with someone who just might have needed it! She turned out to be an absolutely wonderful human being, but by then, friendships were set, and impressions were made, and though we were always friendly, we never became friends. That was on me, and it is a lesson I fight to remember every day – stay open to people who seem to have much more than you do, because everyone has needs, and you might just be able to fulfill one of theirs.

Capitalizing is not just about who you engage with, but also what you do once the connection is made. When someone hands you a business card and says, "Follow up with me tomorrow and let's see how we can work together," you MUST follow up with that person the next day. If you aren't sure how you can work together, ask questions, then listen.

Don't discount what you might bring to the table, and don't wait a week to see if the other person calls you first, or if a better match might come along. It's not dating, it's business and if a better opportunity does come along after, you can always find ways to explore that, too. The point is, you should act immediately when there is an opening for you to advance towards your goals.

If you are at a party and overhear that a developer is looking for businesses to fill a new retail space she's building, and your company would be the perfect fit for that location, be the first person on her call sheet the next day. If someone mentions judging a contest that only has a handful of entries so far, and your product or service meets the criteria, enter right away. Every tiny speck of an advantage should be seized and capitalized on as you pursue success.

Be judicious in how you make use of relationships, but at the same time, don't overly defer to someone else "calling dibs" on an opportunity. In one of my many jobs during college, a co-worker told me that a better position was opening up within our company and he was going to apply for it. I had worked there more than a year longer than he had and knew the job better, so I applied and got it. He was furious, but I was comfortable with my choice because there were several candidates more qualified than he was, and he wouldn't have gotten it regardless of whether or not I applied. Our bosses told him that was the case, but sadly, he never got over what he considered to be my grand betrayal.

In circumstances like these, you have to decide for yourself what your goals are and how fervently you will pursue them. If advancing in your career costs you a friendship, that's okay, as long as you are comfortable in the knowledge that that particular friendship was less important than reaching your goal. Conversely, stay aware of the relationships you're building or destroying, and make careful assessments of whether they may be important to you in the future, and what the consequences may be of damaging them now.

You want to have a network of people who trust you and will go into battle with you, so at times it might be best to put their needs first, but you also want people who support your decisions to pursue whatever it is you need to be successful. If a relationship always requires you to sacrifice your own pursuits to advance the other party, then it may be time to step back and evaluate where it fits into your definitions of success, and how you can reach your goals, either with it or without it. Your job is not to trample on people in a stampede towards some end point, and doing so is likely to harm you more in the long run, but putting personal relationships above your own success – at all costs – is not going to serve you well either.

As I type this, I honestly can't even remember the name of the co-worker who thought I had betrayed him so badly by competing with him for a better job, and taking that job literally changed my life, paying off beyond all expectations over the years. Should I have sacrificed that because someone else wanted it, too? Even if he had been the most qualified candidate before I applied, applying was still the right thing to do, for myself and the company. It is a little sad knowing there is someone out there who probably has negative thoughts about me (if he remembers the incident at all), but I would not change a thing about that choice or the result.

That may sound horrible to some, but in a world where we sometimes must compete with each other for limited opportunities or resources, you will make the occasional enemy. If you can reach all of your goals without doing so, that is amazing and I congratulate you. However, if feelings are hurt or lines get crossed while you advance confidently towards success, you have to accept that and move on. These are tricky waters to navigate, made tougher by not having it come as naturally as it might for someone who was raised speaking Success.

The thing to remember is that you are offering something of value to the world, whether that's your time, your talents, a product you're developing, a service you're providing or some other contribution that needs to be shared for you to be successful. Expanding your circle to include a wider variety of connections and seizing upon any and all advantages is simply your way of making it easier for others to discover what you have that they need. Your success makes the world a better place, ideally, so it is both your prerogative and your obligation to vigorously pursue it. Therefore, you must capitalize!

Reward, verb

> 1. *make a gift in recognition of effort*
> 2. *show appreciation by making a gift*

You won't ever feel successful if you continuously hold your goals at arm's length, never allowing yourself to enjoy the smaller, included achievements on the journey. Build the rewards into your monthly goals, and make those part of what you strive towards. Whatever your most daunting task is, attach the greatest reward to it, and remind yourself of that reward as you make progress. Yes, finishing the task is a reward unto itself, but it can give you an added boost when you give yourself a bonus for what you've done.

It can be a gift for yourself or someone else that you can now buy because you reached a specific goal. It can be five minutes that you take from your day to tell yourself how amazing you are. It can be a whole day off – guilt free – to do something you truly enjoy that you haven't had time for, and when you tie that to a goal achieved, you get to double the pleasure of it.

Pick a goal, and once you achieve it, give yourself a pre-determined reward. Rewards can come in all shapes and sizes. They can be extravagant expenditures that you've been saving up for, or they can be tiny compliments that you give yourself for a job well done, but after the accomplishment, don't skip the reward.

Compare, *verb*

1. *note the similarity or dissimilarity between*
2. *assess the quality of a person or thing as relates to another person or thing*

When my first book, *Happiness as a Second Language*, came out, I struggled with how to market it. I read so many articles, blogs and books, got on every expert's mailing list, joined several indie publishing groups, and through all of this, it always felt like there was so much I was not doing, either because of time constraints or I felt I lacked the skills and resources to do all of what was recommended. No matter what I did, it seemed others were doing more and they were doing it better. Also, sales weren't at the level I was expecting and I was very frustrated and starting to feel like I was failing as an author.

Then, out of the blue, blogger Chris McMullen reached out to me and asked if he could feature my book in a post about how to market nonfiction books. I was stunned.

Why in the world would he ask me when I was doing such a lousy job? But, deciding to capitalize on the opportunity, and trusting Chris, I said, "Sure." He sent me an advance copy of his post about me, and I almost fell out of my chair. It was *so positive*. Despite the fact that I felt I was doing everything wrong, and missing out on a slew of sales, Chris was observing me from the outside and acknowledging all of the things that I was doing right.

Not only was this incredibly affirming, but it also reminded me to stop holding myself to impossible standards and focus my attention on achievable goals. I had to learn how to shut out all of the comparisons to those who seemed to be doing everything I was not. As one of my favorite sayings goes: "Don't compare your behind-the-scenes documentary to someone else's highlight reel." Chris was showing everyone my highlight reel and even I had to admit, it looked pretty good. And I knew it was a struggle behind-the-scenes! In fact, I felt a little bad that the article about my efforts probably made someone else feel exactly as I did – that they were not doing enough.

In pursuing success, lose the verb Compare. There is no reason to compare yourself to anyone else, either to confirm that you are doing better or to worry that you are doing worse. You defined success for yourself, you mapped out your monthly goals, you have actionable daily tasks, so what does anyone else's effort or outcome have to do with that? The only reason to look at what someone else is doing is to see if that person might need your help, or if you can learn from them. Other than that, focus on your actions, your efforts and your outcomes.

Each day, as you make your Count-to-Five list, take a moment to acknowledge what you got accomplished that day, even if it was not everything on your daily to-do list. If an unexpected event popped up that prevented you from moving forward at all, acknowledge that it happened and that you will be back on track as soon as possible. Don't slow in your progress simply because you have slowed in your progress, and if it feels like you aren't getting as far as you'd like, go back to Chapter Three and rework your daily lists and monthly goals to see where you can do more and get better results.

Once you decide on your path to success, the next action is to engage with others to draw them into your journey and help with theirs, and be fully engaged as you work towards your goals. Capitalize on all opportunities that come your way, quickly and with confidence that the world needs what you are offering. Reward yourself as you reach milestones along the way, and don't compare your efforts to anyone else's. You are only competing against the less successful you that would result from not Deciding, Engaging, Capitalizing and Rewarding. Master the conjugation of these verbs and you are well on your way to being fluent in Success.

CHAPTER NINE

THE ADVERBS OF SUCCESS

Almost
Nearly
Barely
Never

An adverb is the part of speech that modifies a verb. In other words, it's the word that describes the action. In most languages, there are adverbs that indicate when something is not quite finished, close to the goal line, just squeaking by or nowhere near enough:

"She has almost completed her degree;"
"They are barely staying in business."

The languages that don't include these words developed in cultures that view the world in a more binary way. Either a thing is or it isn't. There's no concept on your journey of being "almost there" – either you are there or you're not.

Languages from less developed cultures, more survival-based, don't have a need for concepts like striving, attempting, reaching for a goal and being very, very close. If all that your tribe cares about is whether or not they eat tonight, then all that matters is if you killed the gazelle or missed the shot. How far off the target doesn't matter at all. They share Yoda's philosophy: "Do. Or do not. There is no try."

But in any society where people are trying to achieve beyond what was granted them at birth, we must have road markers on the journey. These are the Adverbs of Success.

In the language of Success, these adverbs can be a great help in decision-making. If you know you are *nearly* breaking even, you can start to look at what other resources you can pour into the effort to get to your goal. On the other hand, if you find you are *scarcely* getting anywhere, it may be time to make the decision to move in another direction.

EXERCISE:

RIGHT NOW, LOOK AT where you are on your monthly goals chart and assign an adverb to each of your goals. Are you almost there? Barely there? Did you narrowly achieve that one? This is a great way to decide where to focus your efforts next month. It's okay to back off of one goal if another is so close that one big push gets you there. You just have to be thoroughly honest with yourself – how close or far are you, really?

Always & Never

The two adverbs that pose the biggest threat to your success are *always* and *never*. These pop up in the conversations we have with ourselves all the time, without being subject to the scrutiny they deserve. They are limiting – they limit beliefs, they limit risks and they limit outcomes, and the last thing you need are limiters on your quest for success.

Is it really true that Carla *always* gets the best sales leads, or is Carla doing something you're not to be successful? More likely, all of the reps are getting leads of roughly equal value and Carla is just converting them better. Even more likely, does Carla have some good months and some bad months and because you are still comparing yourself to her, rather than focusing on your own outcomes, you simply see something as "always" happening, when in reality, it happens occasionally, even often, but not always? Think about all of the times you use the word always to describe some event, either happening *for* someone else or *to* yourself, and do an unconditionally honest assessment of whether that's really the case.

An even worse limiter than *always* is *never*. This is the word we use to most limit ourselves. If I truly believe something is never going to happen, then chances are, I'll be right. And as long as I can tell myself it's never going to happen, I'm off the hook for even trying. *Whew!*

Successful people never use the word never when it comes to their goals. They try. And if that doesn't work, they try something else, and if it becomes clear that nothing they are able to do will work, they change direction. They don't look at a thing and say, "That will never happen," without at least an attempt. Several attempts, in fact.

Here's the tricky thing about the word *never* – your brain will go there without you even realizing it, and in the most mundane ways. The good thing is, overcoming this limiter is one of the easiest techniques you can do, with what I call the "Give it a shot!" method.

In other words, if you tell yourself something won't happen, go ahead and give it a shot anyway. After all, if it doesn't work out, you are in the exact position you were in to start with. As long as you haven't spent any irreplaceable resources or burned any bridges getting there, then there was no harm in trying.

Not sure if you are limiting yourself with the word *never*?

Here are three examples of what that behavior looks like in everyday life.

Parking Karma

My dear friend, David, took the most amazing leap by quitting a great paying corporate job to launch Cheltenham Road, a custom woodworking business. His products are gorgeous and not only did they quickly attract a following online, but shops across the country started coming after him to carry his goods. One such shop is a furniture design boutique in downtown Los Angeles, and one day, when he and I had plans to go to lunch, he asked if we could run by there first to drop off some product.

As we got into the vicinity of the shop, he spotted a parking space and started to take it, but I knew that we were still blocks away, and had merchandise to carry, so I asked, "Why aren't we parking closer?" To which David – a master risk-taker and successful businessman said, "There are never any spots closer." So I gave him my most determined stare and said,

"Let's try." As we pulled into the space *directly in front of the shop*, David shot me an annoyed look and said, "This is because of you. If you weren't here, this spot wouldn't be open."

Now, to be fair, there may be some truth to that. I have the world's greatest "parking karma" (meaning I'm very lucky in this area). I got it from my mother, and my sister was blessed with it, too. My husband calls it "Doris Day parking," like in old movies, when Doris Day would just pull up to the building she needed to visit and the space directly in front would be open. In midtown Manhattan. At noon. That happens to me more often than not. It's actually happened to me *in Manhattan.*

But I am fairly certain that I have such great parking karma because I always try to get as close to where I'm going as I can with the belief that I'll get the best spot. Sometimes it doesn't work, and I have to circle the block a few times, and on very rare occasions, I will have passed up a spot that's gone when I go back (but believe me, that is not often).

The best thing about parking karma is that it's contagious. My husband has it now, and even an ex-boyfriend of mine not only has great parking karma, but tells everyone he got it from me, which is true. When he and I were dating, he used to get stressed out about parking before we'd even leave my house. I would always calmly explain that there would be a good spot available and not to worry. Slowly, he started believing me, and eventually he started believing it even when I wasn't in the car, and now, more than a decade later, he still has it. (But don't tell my husband – he likes to think he's the only one...)

Because great parking karma isn't luck, or genetics, it's an attitude. I know I'm going to get a great spot, so I try to get the best spot I can. Usually something is available, and when it's not, I get whatever I can find and stay happy, calm in the knowledge that NOT getting a good spot was the anomaly that day and I'll get better results the next time.

And to really drive the point home – my wood-working friend David has never again parked as far away from the shop as he was going to that day. Now, he tries to get a closer spot every time, and he almost always does. See? Contagious!

The Free Upgrade

Every time I check into a hotel, I ask the clerk, "Is it possible to upgrade me at the same rate?" and the answer is often, "Yes!" (I never leave out the "at the same rate" part, otherwise they are more than happy to upgrade me for more money!)

On a recent trip, as I handed my ID to the clerk and asked my question, the person I was with said, "Oh, they can't do that."

I was stunned. There was no reason for her to speak up at that moment, but worse, it gave the clerk an excuse not to even try, which was a first for me. In the past, even when the answer was no, they at least checked. But he didn't. He shot a dismissive look and said, "We really can't."

I stayed cheerful and polite and asked him to put me in the nicest room available, which at least got a bump to a higher floor, but the whole thing was eye-opening. Not only did my companion limit herself from even the possibility of a nice bonus, but by seeing the world through "never-colored glasses," she had interfered with my success. Mostly, it made me feel sorry for her, since I know the most she will ever get is exactly what she pays for, whereas the rest of us might just get exactly what we ask for.

A Lukewarm Blanket

And one final, fun example of not limiting yourself comes from my friend, Scott, founder of VitalVegas.com, who had an electric blanket that he hated. It never got warm enough, and for a year, every time he used it, he cranked it all the way up to

10 and then sat there, still shivering, cursing himself for buying a bargain blanket.

Then one day, while cranking it to 10, he accidentally went too far and the gauge magically went to 11. He stared at it for a few moments, blinking his eyes, suddenly aware of what might have been the problem with his not-so-hot blanket for the past year. Then, slowly, he reached out and hit the button again. Sure enough, it went to 12. Then 13, 14, 15, 16, 17, 18, 19 and finally H. Presumably for High. He kept pushing, but it did not go above H.

While this could be a lesson for men that every once in a while, reading the instructions might not be such a bad thing, it's also a perfect example of letting the words *always* and *never* limit the outcome without even realizing it. Of course temperature gauges *always* stop at 10, and the highest setting is *never* "H." The warmest it can get is *always* the highest number, which will *never* be more than 10.

Or, you could ask yourself, "Can I make this better?" and just try...

Look around at what you're not satisfied with in your life and ask yourself if you are applying the wrong adverbs to the situation. Are you assuming something is always true, or that something else will never happen, and thus stopping yourself from going for it. Ditch *always* and *never* in your quest to reach your goals, no matter how big or small. Adopt the attitude, "Let me just try first and see if it works."

As hockey legend, Wayne Gretzky says, "You miss 100% of the shots you don't take."

EXERCISE:

THIS WEEK, TRY TO find a better parking space (and really have faith in yourself! Don't keep thinking: "This will fail" the whole time). Then, apply your newfound adverbial attitude to something else. Try to get a lower rate on your cell phone bill or credit card. Try to get booked on that local morning show to discuss your new business. Try to get a meeting with a mentor who you'd truly like to engage. Don't limit yourself with the wrong adverbs. After all, if you try, and get even slightly farther than you would have otherwise, then you succeeded!

Only, Merely, Simply

A common trait among those who lack confidence in their own abilities is what's known as the Imposter Syndrome – the feeling that at any moment, someone is going to walk into your office and announce that you are a fraud. That you don't belong. That no one should be listening to you.

If you have these feelings, don't worry, they are perfectly normal, but you have to work to overcome them. Please trust me when I tell you that everyone else in your workplace is *not* smarter than you. It may feel like others possess not only all of the knowledge and skills that you have, but also more than you'll ever have, but that is not the case. In reality, there are things you are good at and things you're still learning and that makes you like everyone else. No one is coming into your office and calling you a fraud. In fact, they may be afraid that you'll be the one doing that to them.

If you want to overcome the Imposter Syndrome, start by talking about your accomplishments in clear, non-diminishing terms, much like when you were shading your success in the right colors in Chapter Five. Lose the adverbs: *only*, *merely,* and *simply*. You didn't "simply write a proposal," you wrote the proposal that motivated the whole sales team. If someone compliments you for getting a project to the next stage, don't reply with, "I only drew the designs." The person complimenting you knows that you drew the designs and is giving you credit for that being what got it to the next stage. To deny that is to question his intelligence for saying it, and that's just rude. If you get positive feedback, give the speaker respect by accepting it graciously.

There's nothing wrong with being humble, and offering credit to others where due, but this should not happen at the expense of acknowledging your own achievements. No one in the workplace is perfect, and problems arise for everyone, so stay focused, be aware of what you can do and do it.

Don't *merely* do it, just do it.

BONUS ADVERB LESSON: Ruthlessly or Nicely?

Adverbs modify verbs, and if you are looking to engage and capitalize, how do you want to do that – ruthlessly, nicely, aggressively, passively?

The answer is, you want to do that *successfully*, which means all of the above, some of the above or none of the above, depending on the circumstances. If you've listened carefully in all of your encounters with others, and remain focused on the outcome, while ignoring any concern about those judgments that don't affect you, then you are very likely to know exactly what adverbs you need.

To maximize the value of engaging, do it sincerely, thoughtfully and mutually. Don't approach someone asking to, "pick their brain." When you do that, you are announcing that you will receive all of the benefit of the encounter and the other person will get none. It just sounds greedy. Asking for advice is far more polite, and with the request is an implication that the other person may benefit from sharing her insights with you. Also, think of ways to make the encounter mutually beneficial, even if it is as minor as picking up the tab for lunch or coffee. For example, "Can I buy you lunch and get your advice about starting a fashion design business?" is a great way to get some very valuable advice for very little money, and most people like being bought lunch.

Also, keep in mind that those who engage with you are sharing valuable resources, whether their time, their expertise or their contacts, and no one likes to squander their resources. If someone offers you their time, don't waste it by being ill-prepared (or worse – late!). If someone offers to provide a connection between you and another person, you have an obligation to be a good representative of the person who connected you.

Recently, a friend asked me if I could help an acquaintance of his, a singer/actress, find a new manager. As it turned out, I had just met a woman who specialized in managing singers who were transitioning into acting, so I thought it might be a good fit.

I emailed the woman who needed the help and asked her to send me her headshot, resume and links to any content that she thought would be helpful for me to send to the manager. I told her that if she needed to take some time to get videos or her acting reel posted online, that would be fine, there was no hurry. She immediately replied with a one sentence email: "Tell her to look me up on IMDb."

IMDb is the Internet Movie Database, a database of virtually everyone who has ever worked in the entertainment industry. There are more than six million names in it, and this woman has an extremely common one. Just on a lark, I checked and there are 23 different women on IMDb with her same name. But that is beside the point. Once I saw that reply, I was no longer interested in helping her. If she wasn't going to put even the minimum effort into her own success, why should I?

Then, it got worse. A few weeks later, she sent me an email telling me that she hadn't heard from the manager and could I reach out to her again. I replied that I hadn't reached out in the first place, since she never sent me the information I requested. She answered with an angry email, the content of which I honestly cannot recall because I deleted it immediately, but worse, she copied my friend, who first made the request, presumably believing that he should know that I had not helped her.

He sent me a deeply apologetic email, asking that I not judge him based on her behavior. I assured him that my affection for him was too genuine to ever let her lack of professionalism alter it, but thanked him for understanding why I chose not to do anything else on his friend's behalf.

Unless she reads this book and changes her ways, that woman will not be successful. She put someone else's relationship in jeopardy and frittered away a potentially valuable contact by engaging with both of us selfishly, lazily and thoughtlessly (three adverbs that will not lead to success) and by failing to stay focused on the outcome.

CHAPTER TEN

The Negative Form

Nein

아니다

いいえ

нет

Não

Non

In how many languages can you say the word, "No?"

Chances are, quite a few. It is one of the easiest words to grasp and remember, and no matter what your need for learning the language – business, travel, to pass the 10th grade – you need to use "No" often.

The exact opposite is true in the language of Success. In this language, the word "No" is one of the most difficult to master, and you do not want to use it unless absolutely necessary.

"No" can end conversations, halt progress, offend potential supporters and close off a host of options. On the other hand, "No" can protect from failure, prevent time wasting or avoid distractions. "No" can make you happy, as you release yourself from a burden, or dampen your spirits as you turn down an attractive offer because you don't have the time, money or freedom to take advantage of it.

How and When NOT to say "No"

In almost all business dealings, try to avoid using the word, "no" entirely. You can still be rejecting the other side's proposition, but as long as you don't come right out and say, "no," the door is open to reach an outcome that both sides will feel is a victory, or at least less of a compromise.

One of my Happiness coaching clients owns a piece of property that is part of a larger parcel being considered for development by the government as a public facility. The property owners have a chief negotiator representing them, and my client has gotten the equivalent of a Masters degree in Negotiating simply by being in a room with this man for the past few years. Imagine an undertaking with more than a dozen parties, including politicians, bureaucrats, unions, construction companies, vendor representatives, property owners, environmental protection advocates and more, all of whom have different agendas.

The property owners' agenda is to make sure that: (1) their property is selected as the site for development; (2) they maximize the price they get; and (3) they don't have to pay anything out of pocket to make this happen. Every time one of these goals meets with resistance from any other party, the negotiator simply takes a new approach. He brings different people to the table, he finds precedent that allows him to ask for something in a way that aligns with everyone's comfort levels, or he simply steps back and waits patiently until the obstacle clears itself out of the way, which happens often.

When my client was telling me about all the various things this negotiator has achieved in the years that they've been working on it (and it still has many years to go, because that's what developments of this magnitude require), he said, "The guy is amazing, he never gives 'No' for an answer."

That statement took me a bit by surprise and I replied, "What?"

Laughing, my client quickly corrected himself, "I mean he never takes 'No' for an answer."

But it was such a profound slip that I had to stop him, so we could really examine the ramifications of what he'd accidentally said. As we delved into it, it became more and more clear that his mistake was accurate – the negotiator never *gives* "no" for an answer. No matter what is being asked of him, he finds a way to make the asker feel like they are getting what they want, or he gets them to change what they are asking for. He never just says, "No."

I wish I had understood and mastered this skill earlier in my screenwriting career. My first job as a screenwriter was adapting the novel, *Social Crimes*, for Phoenix Pictures, with Joel Schumacher attached to direct the film. *Social Crimes* is a dark revenge tale about a woman whose husband drops dead after 30 years of marriage and he leaves all his money to his mistress, leaving the widow penniless at the age of 50.

Joel and I worked on the outline together, then he went off to produce and direct the film version of *Phantom of the Opera*, and I set about to writing the script. I turned in my first draft to Phoenix Pictures, and in my one and only notes meeting with Mike Medavoy, the founder and head of the company, the conversation went like this:

Mike Medavoy: "Could this be reworked to be a vehicle for, say...Reese Witherspoon?"
(It was 2003. Reese Witherspoon was 27 years old.)
Valerie: "To play the mistress? It's such a small part, I don't think she'd take it."
Mike Medavoy: "To play the wife."
Valerie: "No. She's too young."

The meeting ended shortly after that, without me realizing that I had probably just killed my movie, or at least my opportunity to continue writing it. What I learned afterwards was how this whole movie project even came into being, which explained that conversation.

It turns out that a year before that fateful meeting, Reese Witherspoon was shopping a movie version of the novel, *Vanity Fair,* for herself to star in, which Mike Medavoy wanted to produce. She chose to make it with a different company instead, and while Mike was discussing missing out on that project with his friend, Joel Schumacher, Joel said, "You should make *Social Crimes.* It's a modern day *Vanity Fair.*"

What Joel must not have understood was that Mike Medavoy didn't want a *Vanity Fair* project, he wanted a Reese Witherspoon project. He had won the rights to the book *Social Crimes* in a bidding war against Goldie Hawn. Perhaps this should have been a sign to everyone that it wasn't an ideal vehicle for Reese Witherspoon. It also would have been helpful if we'd all been told that that was the goal in the first place – create something that will attract Reese Witherspoon as its star.

I can't say with certainty that this is the reason the project died. The executive overseeing the movie parted ways with Phoenix Pictures just as the option for the rights to the book expired and no one at the company renewed them in time, which gave the book's author the chance to reclaim them and she did. Mike had sent the script to her and she was furious because Joel and I had changed the ending substantially from the book's – so much so that it would have killed her intended franchise. I can't imagine how she would have felt seeing Reese Witherspoon play her 50 year-old heroine.

A few years later, when I signed with Paradigm for representation, I told that story to my new agent, Lucy Stille, who was the only person ever to say to me, "You could have made that work for Reese Witherspoon. You should have."

She was right. And even if I could not have made the script work, I should have never used the word, "no" in that meeting. What I should have said was, "Let me think about that," then gone back to everyone else involved and figured out why I was being asked about Reese Witherspoon. If I'd done that, I might be a more successful screenwriter today.

If something is being asked of you, do everything in your power to figure out what the party asking really needs, what the agenda may be, and how you can achieve the outcome you seek without ever using the word, "No."

"Yes, and..."

The first day of almost any improvisational acting class involves everyone getting up and trying to create something out of nothing. Usually, the exercise involves a game known as, "Yes, and..."

The rule of this game is that every person has to accept whatever someone else on stage comes up with. If the performers are doing a scene set on the International Space Station and someone announces that he's playing a horse, they just have to go with it. They have to say, "Yes, (you're a horse), and..." then they have to come up with an elaboration that incorporates a horse into the performance and finds a way to make it work. Saying, "No, you're not a horse," kills the possibility for an even more creative, fun and successful scene.

For years now, this game has been part of business school orientations and corporate team-building outings, because at some point, leaders in those organizations realized how much could be achieved by forcing everyone to listen to whatever any team member was bringing to the table and seeing if it could work into the solutions they were coming up with.

It's far easier to say, "No," in a meeting, especially if you're the one running it and there's limited time, but that allows ease and efficiency to trump effectiveness. If you establish a "no" culture, people will choose not to participate at all, which might eliminate the best input. Also, by forcing yourself to say, "Yes, and..." you become a better listener, which, as we've already covered, is a very important component to being successful in any relationship, whether at work or otherwise.

"No" shuts everyone down, and "Yes" invites them in. Don't be afraid of "Yes," especially if you are in charge. As much as possible, when supervising a team, embrace "Yes" and dismiss "No" and see how it makes those reporting to you flourish.

In my life, when I have succeeded, it's been for many different reasons, but when I failed it was always for the same reason. I said "Yes" when I should have said "No."

– speaker unknown

Once again, I must include a quote without attribution, as there appears to be no definitive source for the originator of this one. The possibilities range from Warren Buffett or Richard Branson to Abraham Lincoln. I'm pretty sure it wasn't Honest Abe.

That said, the point is the same – don't be afraid to say, "No," when necessary to maintain your pursuit of success. The tricky part is knowing when saying "No" is to your advantage and when it isn't.

Here are some potential situations to think about how, or if, you'd say, "No."

1. You were invited to speak for free at a small conference, several hours from your home.

2. Your supplier has offered you a huge discount on your order if you'll fudge the prices so that she can pay less taxes.

3. You just signed with the largest literary agency in town and a friend wants you to submit his script to your agent.

4. Your married boss wants the two of you to have a non-business dinner together, and possibly more.

5. An acquaintance just found out you have expertise in an area where she is starting a business and she wants you to partner with her, even though you left that field.

6. The impossible project that no one in the company has been able to effectively manage has been offered to you.

1. You were invited to speak for free at a small conference, several hours from your home.

It is incredibly tempting to accept every offer that comes your way, particularly when you are first starting out, but each opportunity brings with it an opportunity cost, which is the value of what you are giving up by accepting this offer.

Many factors have to go into deciding whether or not to say, "No." Will you be paid anything, even something in trade, and if so, will it be close to your standard speaking rate? How many people will be in attendance and are any of them solid potential clients or connections for you? Will this event lead to booking other, larger events? How much will it cost you to go, in terms of travel and time? How much time will you need to prepare, and will the prepared material be something that can be repurposed for other events? Did you make a commitment to yourself to no longer accept unpaid work, and do you intend to stick with it?

Using your best judgment, if your answers to these questions leads you to realize that saying, "Yes," is not to your advantage, feel free to politely decline. There is great power in knowing your value and saying, "No," when what you will be getting is less than what you are giving. Once you say, "No," do not second guess yourself. In the next chapter, we'll discuss how to walk away from regret, but for now, know that delivering a firm "No," when it's in your best interest, is one of the most empowering, success-oriented decisions you can make.

2. Your supplier has offered you a huge discount on your order if you'll fudge the prices so that she can pay less taxes.

Tempting offers like this will come your way often when running your own business, or even while working for someone else. There are plenty of people in the world who said, "Yes" to an offer like this and never gave it a second thought, with no negative outcomes. However, minimum security prisons have plenty of residents who would gladly tell you not to make this choice. In this case, you look at the supplier and say, "I'd appreciate the best discount you can give me without having anything inaccurate or untrue on the paperwork. Thanks."

You may come from a background or community where it feels like the only people who get ahead are the ones who scam and cheat. If that's all you've ever seen, then it might not even be clear what is right and wrong in this situation. Your challenge is to decide *how* you want to reach your goals. It may be harder or seem to take longer following a path without deceit, duplicity or moral ambiguity, but if you included integrity as part of your definition of success, as discussed in Chapter Six, then your choices are much easier.

If something feels wrong to you, don't do it. Even if it seems like it's easier to just go along, you will find that in the long run, it almost never is. It is far easier to live with the twinge of doubt that might result from doing the right thing than the enormous regret that might accompany the consequences of doing the wrong thing. And if you need to break the law to be successful in your chosen field, then maybe it's time to start exploring a different field.

3. You just signed with the largest literary agency in town and a friend wants you to submit his script to your agent.

One week after I was signed by Creative Artists Agency (CAA, at the time, the most powerful agency in town), a friend asked me to give his script to my agent, and stupidly, I did. I wanted to be helpful. I thought I had "made it" and I wanted to give someone else a boost up.

The thing is, I hadn't made it. Not even close. I had sold a couple of scripts that got CAA's attention, but had not earned any money for the agency yet. In fact, asking my new agent to read my friend's script was one of the first conversations we had after he signed me, and it was a glaring error in judgment.

In this case, the "No" is very simple. What I should have said was: "I'm sorry, I'm really not in a position to do that yet. I'll be happy to help once I've sold a few more projects and earned fees my agents can commission." You always want to help other people advance in their careers when you can, but only from a place of actually being able to help. Be honest with yourself and others about what you are really capable of, and don't jeopardize your own advancement by doing a favor which ultimately will not help either of you.

4. Your married boss wants the two of you to have a non-business dinner together, and possibly more.

Workplace affairs almost never advance careers, and often leave a swath of destruction for everyone in their wake, usually far worse for the underling in the situation. If you've never worked in an office, and were not raised with an awareness of these kinds of group dynamics, you may not realize how toxic it can be to be the subject of office gossip. Not only does it harm you in that workplace, but it can follow you for years to come, particularly now, in the information age, when every indiscretion is public and lives in search engines forever.

Throughout your career, in any workplace, you are going to want to avoid being "on everybody's tongue." Don't do anything that might make it harder on yourself, like sleeping with the boss. In this case, a simple "No thank you." will suffice. If there is more pressure beyond that, say, "I appreciate any mentorship and work assistance you can provide to me, but I am not entering into a personal relationship with you. Thank you for understanding and accepting that."

If the problem persists, your options are to go to Human Resources, go to a lawyer, go find a new job or just keep saying, "No," until someone finally accepts it. Just don't say, "Yes." It will not be worth it.

5. An acquaintance just found out you have expertise in an area where she is starting a business and she wants you to partner with her, even though you are no longer in that field.

This may be the opportunity you have been waiting for, or it may feel like a step backwards, even if you know you'd flourish in the role.

You do not want this to be one of those situations where you made the wrong choice simply out of fear or a sense of obligation. If you choose to accept an offer like this, remember to constantly monitor your monthly goals, see how this fits into your choices and don't be afraid to change direction if this venture is not escalating you towards your own definition of success.

Use your gut. And your brain. And everything you've learned up to now. If it seems that someone in your life or your workplace is taking you farther from your own pursuit of success, then, without guilt or apology, focus on your outcome and give a friendly, but firm, "No." Your friend will either understand or choose not to, which you can't control.

6. The impossible project that no one in the company has been able to effectively manage has been offered to you.

Why has no one been able to manage this beast? Is it structured to be unwinnable? If so, think about whether or not you want to be its next victim. This requires ruthless self-assessment. Carefully examine what you will bring to the project and what you will get out of it. Be totally honest with yourself. Don't just look at the upside if everything works out perfectly, but look at all the potential outcomes, and include the opportunity costs of what you may be giving up if you say, "Yes."

You may wind up the conquering hero, if you can succeed where every other party has failed. There may be no consequences to failure, since everyone knows the reality of it. Your ego may be screaming to give this a shot, so you'd regret turning it down more than you'd regret the potential failure. In that case, go for it. Say, "Yes, I'll do it!" But take the time to make sure what you choose is best for both you and the company, primarily for you, and if you must say, "No, thank you," find a career-advancing way to do so.

If You Just Don't Know, Don't Just Say, "No."

Finally, I leave you with the dumbest use of the word, "No" ever.

When I first arrived in Hollywood, I knew nothing about the film business and decided that I had to get on movie sets to learn what it's all about, so I signed with a service that provides background extras for film and television. My very first movie as an extra also happened to be George Clooney's first movie as a Director, *Confessions of a Dangerous Mind*.

The scene I was to be an extra in was set in the Coney Island amusement park in the early 60s. I was costumed in an impossibly cute, strapless dress and low-heeled pumps, with full hair and make-up, and there was no mistaking that I was supposed to be in front of the camera.

There were about 100 extras, and to make it look like a real boardwalk, some of the girls were carrying balloons and some had stuffed animals and several were supposed to be carrying cotton candy. Big fluffy cones of cotton candy. Unfortunately, none of the prop guys really knew how to use the cotton candy machine to create perfect pink clouds on a stick. Run it too hot, and instead of gossamer sugar floss you get sticky pink goo. Twirl too slowly or too long, you scorch one side, or the cone collapses, or any other thing that yields an ugly blob.

I know this because I worked at the Great America amusement park for four summers, and three of those summers were spent making cotton candy.

It was very damp that evening, so these cones didn't last long between takes, meaning fresh ones had to be made every few minutes. After watching several rounds of frustration and anger on the part of the crew, I walked over and volunteered to do it. I guess cotton candy is like riding a bike, because the first one looked okay, but by the second one, they were picture perfect. Literally.

After each take, a prop person would walk among the extras, decide who needed her puff of sugar replaced, and send her over to me. The cotton candy machine was on an elevated platform, so I had to climb a ladder in my super cute dress and low-heeled pumps and spin fresh pink floss. It was so much fun!

This went on for a few hours, and at one point, a crew member who was clearly in charge (probably the Assistant Director or the Production Manager) came over and saw me on the ladder and started screaming. The prop guys quickly explained that I was the only one who really knew how to operate the contraption, and by the way, hadn't he noticed how great all the cotton candy looked? He stared back and forth between them and me, then finally gave in. He looked at someone and said, "Okay. Get her a prop voucher," then he turned to me and said, "You want a prop voucher?"

I had no idea what that meant, and instead of asking, I just said, "No, I don't need that." And he shrugged and said, "Fine," and walked away. Here's the thing – vouchers are essentially union pay slips. Getting one would have meant being paid as a prop specialist (the designation for people with specific skills) instead of as a background extra. I have since been told that prop departments don't use vouchers, so the Assistant Director or Production Manager or whoever he was should have asked a different question, but the question wasn't the problem, the answer was.

If you just don't know, don't just say, "No."

As an extra that day, I made $54. As a prop specialist, I would have made $350 and been credited in the movie. I also would have earned a "union day," which would have been useful if I ever wanted to do more work in that field. Saying, "No, I don't need that," is probably one of the most boneheaded things I've ever done.

And yet, it wasn't even the most boneheaded thing I did that day. Later that evening, because I was not focused on the outcome of my actions, I got an even greater opportunity than getting a voucher for a $350 payday, and I blew it even worse. George Clooney, standing three feet away, turned and asked me a question I wasn't prepared for and I completely bungled my reply. That story is discussed in the next chapter, on the Past, Present and Future Tense of Success.

CHAPTER ELEVEN

SUCCESS –
THE "PAST IMPERFECT" TENSE

I was successful
I am successful.
I was not successful.
I will be successful.

Every language has an algorithm for talking about what is happening right now (in the present tense), what happened yesterday (past tense) or what will happen tomorrow (future tense). This is one of the more complex things to learn in a new language, because for every rule, there are a dozen or so exceptions that you have to memorize to converse successfully in this language.

In the language of Success, luckily, these tenses are much simpler to grasp and absorb. The past does not govern you, the present is all you have to work with, and the future is what you are striving for. If you keep those three maxims in mind at all times, Success will be much easier to master.

The rules here are simple: (1) don't let the success that you lacked (or achieved) in the past weigh down your ability to decide, engage and capitalize now; (2) don't discount future success as something you may not attain; and (3) live and act in the present, staying fully engaged at all times.

The "Past Imperfect" Tense

One of the great challenges to your success is the belief that something you did in the past is keeping you from being successful today, or that if you had made a different decision then, your life would be so much better now. This is the "past imperfect" tense in the language of Success, and you should fight like hell to never use it. It will not advance you confidently towards your goals. Poor choices in the past are only good for the lessons gained from them, and once those lessons are learned, lose any other thought of what was possible then or what could be now.

In the spring of 1995, I had to make the difficult decision of whether to stay at Berkeley, complete my Ph.D., and pursue my dream of becoming an economics professor, or leave school to begin practicing law, earning twice as much that first year as I would four years later, after finishing my dissertation. I used to joke that it didn't take a Ph.D. in economics to make that choice.

But maybe it did. The study of economics is about the consequences of decisions – the intended and unintended effects of changes in direction. Was I really measuring all of the tangibles and intangibles in my decision, and giving enough (or any) credence to the unknown, to the opportunity cost of the path not taken?

I loved practicing law. As much as I hated law school, I discovered with my summer job at a big firm in Chicago that the actual work of being a lawyer was nothing like school, and for my tastes, far more rewarding. Leaving the Ph.D. program to do that full time was a no-brainer. Plus, I was getting paid more than I had ever imagined. At 26, I was able to buy a house and five years later I'd paid off my student loans. How could practicing law not be the better choice?

Except that my abandoned dissertation was on the game theory failures of the 1993 NBA draft, which was a topic that incorporated everything I loved – economics, game theory and college basketball. I never thought much about what life would have held if I'd finished it, but a few years ago, I was discussing the topic with a friend who said, "Can you imagine if you'd written that? Every team in the NBA would have come after you as a consultant for the draft."

Honestly, I had never thought about it. My belief was always that finishing the economics degree would have meant becoming a professor, nothing more. Being a professor would have also been a great life. I love teaching, particularly at the university level, and the lifestyle is far more humane than that of lawyers or investment bankers. In fact, it's comparable to screenwriters, but with far more job security. I just never imagined anything could have turned out better than what I chose – lawyer, banker, executive, screenwriter, director, author, speaker, coach. These have all been rewarding careers, with varying degrees of financial return, and yet, this new thought that a different path could have been equally enriching also intrigued me. I never regretted my choice, but for the first time, I understood how I might have.

Thinking about an alternate life based on different choices in the past is fun, as long as it is just a brief diversion, and doesn't turn into regret. That's easy to say when the choices you've made haven't led to disaster or ruin. Anyone who believes themselves to be successful can always look back and say, "Yes, I made all the right choices for myself."

The difficulty is when you are not where you want to be, and have specific choices in the past that you can look to and tell yourself that life would have been better if you'd just gone left instead of right at a particular crossroad. The reality is – you have no way of knowing. It may be that the seemingly bad decision or turn of fortune in the past is the thing that paves the way for some future success beyond your wildest dreams. Even if that is so, it is almost impossible to see the connection while in the middle of it, especially before you've reached that peak.

In the book, *Happiness as a Second Language*, I share the story about not getting into an economics graduate program directly out of college (the path I had always planned), which is the reason I went to law school in the first place. At the time, I was devastated, but in hindsight, that led to a far superior outcome. I call this the "future uncertain" tense in the language of Happiness – the fact that the bad thing happening to you now may be the best thing that ever happens to you, so just wait it out, continue to stay positive, make good choices, and see where it leads.

In the language of Success, the "past imperfect" tense is comparable. You have no way of knowing if the different choice you could have made in the past would have resulted in a better outcome, so don't dwell on it. Do not behave as if that other choice was perfect. Regret is one of the most disabling verbs you can saddle yourself with, so dump it as quickly and completely as possible.

If you have no regrets over past events in your life, then that's great. You are ready to start working on success in the present and looking towards the future. However, if you feel held back by, or burdened with, regret then take some time to release it.

EXERCISE:

THINK OF THE CHOICE you regret from your past that you are trying to release, and imagine the worst possible outcomes had you taken the unchosen route. Really get creative. Have fun with this. You have to train your brain to realize that the road not taken would not have been better, and allow yourself to let go of the past, live in the present and focus on the future.

For example, if you dropped out of medical school, paint a picture of yourself becoming a doctor, getting pressure from a friend to write illegal prescriptions and winding up in jail, where all sorts of bad things happen to you. If this seems ridiculous, then chances are you aren't being crippled by regret. Those who are must find a way to get past the past, and even laugh about it. Do you regret mouthing off to your boss in that meeting, which ultimately got you fired? Imagine that you stayed in that job and the following year they put you in charge of a new division in a country where you were then kidnapped and tortured for ransom. Imagine your worst nightmare coming true as a result of having done what you are now punishing yourself for not doing. That's how you shake the shackles of past mistakes or failures.

Get a solid grasp of how much worse off you could be than you are now. The rosy picture you are painting of how life would have gone had you made the right choice is just as much a fantasy as the grim picture you just created, so tell yourself the grim one is the truth and let it all go.

The only way to actively pursue success is to be present at all times in your life today. During your quiet moments, reflect deeply on why you made the choices that you did, and if there is something in you that needs to change to make better choices now, work on changing it. But don't spend more than ten seconds wishing you had a time machine, because you don't.

Growing as a person, on the other hand, is a form of time travel. It allows you to mentally go back to the past, see what you need to fix, and use that knowledge to alter the future. Take the lessons from the past without losing time in the present lamenting them. That is how you speak Success in the future.

And here is the story about George Clooney that I promised in the last chapter. This is the one tale of regret that I still flash to every now and then, wondering if life would have been radically different had I been prepared for my big moment with the man. This is the thing I did on set that day that was even more boneheaded than refusing a significantly higher pay rate because I didn't want to admit that I didn't understand what a prop voucher was.

As I shared, I was working as a background extra (and cotton candy maker) on the set of *Confessions of a Dangerous Mind*. By sheer luck, and dress size at the time, I was costumed in one of the cutest dresses ever made. Strapless with a cinched waist and a flared skirt, black with little pink martini glasses, it gave me more of an hourglass figure than I've ever had. Every other girl on set remarked that I had the best dress. Without doubt, I did.

That morning, production assistants told all of the 100 extras to go to "hair, then makeup." When I went to the hair trailers, the line was insanely long, so I just decided to go straight to makeup instead. Since I was the only one there, and wearing a far superior costume, the makeup artists assumed I was some featured actress, so they spent 45 minutes doing my makeup. (I heard from the other extras that they got about 5-10 minutes each.)

I then went to the hair trailer, and by then, everyone else had cleared out, so once again, I got very special treatment. Keep in mind, this was my first time on a movie set. I had no idea that this was not normal.

We all went to the holding area for "background per-formers" (a.k.a., extras), then were called to set, placed, given instructions and run through the scene several times. It was then time to shoot it, and that's when we first saw the director, George Clooney. He called for action, we shot one take, and he decided that the scene would look better if it took place at night, so we were sent back to the holding area to wait four hours for the sun to go down. That meant dinner and possibly overtime. The extras were ecstatic.

Four hours later, we were again called to set and placed. We shot several takes and it was really fun. In between, I was making cotton candy and just enjoying the moment, except it was winter (or what passes for winter in Los Angeles) and we were all freezing. Someone from the crew told anyone who had a jacket that they could go get it, and they offered blankets to anyone who might need one.

Luckily, I had brought a sweater with me that day. A giant, bulky, cardigan sweater that covered every inch of my super-cute dress, and which I stretched over my hands and held tightly closed at the base of my neck to try to stay warm, when not spinning cotton candy. Yep, I sure was lucky to have that!

Then, we got to the point in the shooting schedule where Sam Rockwell, the film's lead actor, was needed in the scene, so he came to set and some crew members started weaving among the extras. One of them pointed at me and said, "You." He waved me over and I followed him to the spot near the cameras where Sam Rockwell was standing. Two other women and I were placed right next to the star of the movie. That's when George Clooney came over and started giving him direction.

This was what I was there for! To learn how a movie set works. To watch a real director working with real actors and now I had a front row seat. I just stared at the two of them, not more than three feet from me, and I hung on every word. That's when George Clooney glanced over and noticed me, standing there, slack-jawed, not in the world's cutest dress with the special-attention hairdo and the 45-minute makeup job, but instead, hunched into an oversized cardigan wrapped tightly under my chin, shivering.

He said, "You cold?"

I suddenly realized I had been spoken to. What came out of my mouth sounded something like, "Hyunh?" So George Clooney repeated the question, slowly, so that the brain-addled extra who couldn't possibly be a former securities lawyer/investment banker could understand it. "Are. You. Cold?"

It finally registered that he was, in fact, speaking to me, and I was, in fact, cold, so I desperately tried to say, "Yes" (which was a stupid answer to begin with), and it came out, "Yee-ee-uh-hunh." He nodded and walked away. Two seconds later, the crew member who first moved me next to Sam Rockwell came over and told me to go back to my original spot. That was it. Lesson in filmmaking over.

When I relive that event in my memory, the moment when George looks at me and asks, "You cold?" I smile sweetly, reply, "Of course not," stand up straight, peel off my bulky sweater to reveal my amazing dress and say, "I'm ready to go. What do you need?"

That would have been such a better choice! So now, in my *let-go-of-the-past* imagination, after I give George Clooney the absolutely perfect answer at that moment, all kinds of horrible things happen. I wind up the subject of vicious tabloid rumors and am forced to move back to Indiana, never having sold a screenplay, unable to make it in this cut-throat business. My name becomes the butt of industry jokes, so I change it. Because of my notoriety, I can't resume practicing law, so I start waiting tables at the Waffle House off I-65, hoping no one recognizes me and that TMZ is not outside whenever I get off work. I never return to Hollywood. I never marry. I eventually get a cat. Multiple cats. And I hate cats.

Now that's how you demolish regret.

CHAPTER TWELVE
THE GARB OF SUCCESS

Ma chemise
Meine Jacke
내 치마

I never intended to include a chapter in this book about clothing. While learning all of the articles of clothing is one of the basic vocabulary lessons in any new language, it did not seem a significant enough factor in a quest for success to require examination here.

Yet, as I wrote more and more of this book, recounting times when people (myself included) failed or hit setbacks for things that were perfectly within our control, I noticed how many of the stories were about the clothing, and more importantly, how the way that clothing affects how others see us. I learned all of those lessons the hard way, and if writing this means someone else doesn't have to, then it's worth including.

If you're raised a Kennedy, you probably know exactly when to wear a suit and when to wear gym shoes. You know what kind of suit to buy (color, cut, brand) and how to keep it clean and presentable without ruining it. You know how to accessorize and groom for maximum effect.

Does it seem odd to include the word "groom" here? It's not. Different cultures have different standards when it comes to personal hygiene, and what might be instinctive to you, like washing a soiled shirt before wearing it again, or using deodorant every day, might be a foreign language to someone whose family has only ever performed agricultural work in an underdeveloped economy.

No matter what career you want, how you present yourself matters. Some might balk at this, but it is absolute fact, and you ignore it at your peril. Take the time to observe the people who are successful in your chosen field. What do they wear? How do they appear? Do the women all wear comfortable shoes every day, or are heels and hose the norm? Is the man running the sales department clean shaven, or does he look like he just rolled out of bed after a 3-day weekend? How put together is the top performer? That should be your target and your goal. This has nothing to do with your performance or how capable you are at your job, but it is a part of how your overall performance is evaluated, and if your success requires others to approve, support and promote you through the ranks, then why hinder your success with the wrong facade?

If dressing the part requires resources beyond your current state, do what it takes to get the clothes, shoes, accessories and grooming supplies you need to be a contender. Look into local charities that provide "career closets" for men and women. Shop at thrift stores and ask the employees to help you find the most presentable looks. Skip a dinner out once a week and put that money aside for a designer suit or a workplace-appropriate manicure. Ask for clothing store gift cards for birthdays or graduation. Consult professional magazines for your industry to see how the people in the pages are dressed, and figure out how to put together similar looks with what is already in your closet.

If eighty people show up for an interview, don't be one of the many who get easily eliminated because your shirt is a wrinkled mess or your shoes aren't right for your suit. As Coco Chanel said, "Dress sloppily and they notice the clothes, dress impeccably and they notice the person."

Here are six stories of clothes, shoes and accessories making a difference, just from my own experience and that of my friends. I'm sure if I opened up the floor for input, dozens more would quickly flow in.

#1 – Even What You Wear Underneath Matters

At my law firm in San Francisco, we had an assistant who returned to work in her fifties after her long career as a wife ended abruptly, and not by her choice. She was assigned to a young, male attorney and became devoted to him, like the son she wished she had. He took advantage of this, asking and allowing and eventually expecting her to perform all kinds of personal errands that were well beyond her job description.

By chance, I happened to overhear the conversation that took place outside my office when two of the other assistants asked the office manager to step in and put a stop to this. It was long overdue, and the office manager agreed to talk to both of them. I'll never forget one assistant's final words as the office manager started to walk away. She said, "And while you're at it, tell her to stop wearing those thick, dime-store hose. It embarrasses the whole firm."

I'm not sure if that was said loudly for my benefit or not, but I knew it applied to me, too. I went home that night and threw out every pair of L'eggs I owned. Until that day, I had no idea anyone would ever notice what kind of stockings I was wearing or that it could possibly matter, but mine were very inexpensive, and clearly it did.

#2 – All Suits Are Not Created Equal

My dear friend, Steven, is one of the biggest go-getters I have ever known. Through sheer tenacity, he got into the broker training program at Merrill Lynch long after the hiring and interview process for that year had closed. Steven didn't come from a Wall Street background, and even though his family was financially successful, they still didn't prepare him for one key aspect of his new job: the business suits.

Steven owned a beautiful seersucker suit that he made the mistake of wearing into the office one day. If you don't know what this is, do a quick image search online. Now picture every big time banker, broker and dealmaker you've ever seen in the news, on TV, in movies or being indicted. Can you picture any of them in seersucker?

As soon as his boss saw him that morning, he exclaimed, "What the hell is this? You came to work in your pajamas today? Get out. Go home." Steven asked if he should change and come back and the boss said no, he was being docked a day. The trainee program only allowed two absences in the first six months, and this cost him one of them. It was a huge deal.

I was still in law school at the time, and when he told me the story, I was appalled. I thought the boss was completely in the wrong, but now, in hindsight, I see things differently.

One can look around any room in high finance and know that a seersucker suit is not going to fit in, just as a tuxedo wouldn't fit in, or a cheap polyester sports coat, or anything a small-town photographer keeps on hand for senior class pictures. If a client comes in that day, and your outfit makes her question the judgment of the whole firm, that's a risk your employer can't afford. Steven's boss was right to be that much of a jackass that day, because the message was loud, clear and unmistakable. Every industry has its dress code, and violations are rarely tolerated.

Pay attention to what succeeds in your workplace, and until you are at the very top, and it no longer matters, don't let your clothes be what people remember about you.

#3 – The Judgment of Inferiors

At my investment bank, there was a horrible little person who I will just call M who made me miserable. She had been a corporate finance analyst there for three years when I was hired as an associate, which meant I was senior to her, something she could barely stomach. The fact that I had two years of practicing law and two advanced degrees that she did not mattered not a bit to M, and worse, she was assigned to teach me all of our forms and models, which are unique to each bank and take time to learn.

Despite her unpleasant attitude, I went out of my way to be nice to her, and one day, she walked in my office wearing new shoes that looked great. I said, quite pleasantly (with not a bit of snark or sarcasm), "Oh, look at your beautiful shoes and nice pedicure." She replied (and if it's possible to imagine the nastiest tone of voice you can, you still aren't hearing how caustic this was): "Well, it's *classless* to wear open-toed shoes without painted toenails."

As you can imagine, I was sitting there, open-toed shoes, blank toenails and all. That was the day I decided I never had to care about her opinion or treat her with any excess respect again. I also decided to put more effort into my appearance. I refuse to ever allow myself to be judged by someone like M again, and had to acknowledge that if she felt that way, some of my superiors might as well, which was a risk I wasn't willing to take.

#4 – The Care and Feeding of Fine Garments

Riding in a cab with another investment banker, I made a comment about getting my suit dry cleaned. He asked if I'd spilled something on it and I said no, I just wore it. He explained to me that business suits are rarely cleaned, only pressed, provided you didn't perspire profusely in them, and that a good suit should last 20 years, even with regular wearing.

I had no idea. I was getting my suits cleaned every other time I wore them, and was very disappointed that they were getting so shiny so quickly (a bad trait for a good suit). The cleaners should have told me, but they didn't, and again, I wasn't raised in a family of suit-wearers.

Shower daily. Try not to sweat. Shirts get laundered. Suits get pressed. Sometimes just steamed, but only rarely dry-cleaned.

Who knew?

#5 – If You Want the Part, Look the Part

The first time I went out for TV staffing in Hollywood (the meetings writers have with network executives, studios and executive producers to try to get on the writing staff of a television series), I dressed like it was a corporate job interview. My agents and managers had no idea. They nearly killed me when they found out.

My writing had gotten me a lot of meetings, and often I'd meet with everyone from the network executives all the way up to the showrunner, but I never got the gig, which mystified everyone. Luckily, one showrunner was candid with my manager about it. He said, "I want writers who look like writers, not writers who look like lawyers."

The funny thing was, I knew how television writers are supposed to look. If you watch the show "30 Rock," that is pretty much exactly what television writers look like and I should have dressed the part. It just felt weird to go on a job interview wearing jeans and a tee-shirt. But that's what I should have done.

And that show I didn't get hired on – it was about lawyers!

#6 – Can a Purse Really Matter That Much?

To me, the purpose of a purse is to carry everything I need and if it matches what I'm wearing, that's a good day. The idea of spending more than $30 on one was as ludicrous as putting that money in a shredder. I never imagined being judged in a career like law or finance by the quality of the purse I was carrying. And yet, I was.

I'm practical and could not understand what in the world would be worth the kind of money my colleagues were paying for their purses. I didn't realize the message one sends with a high-end handbag.

My friend, Shari, a successful attorney in Manhattan, stayed with me for a week while visiting San Francisco, and about a week later, a box arrived in the mail with a lovely thank you gift – an adorable Coach purse.

This was something I never would have bought for myself, but I could not deny the quality of it, and frankly, I loved that little purse. The first day I carried it to the office, I happened to get on the elevator with the only female Managing Director at my bank and she immediately said, "Oh, is that the new Coach bag? Can I see it?" We bonded over the purse, and after that, we spoke often in the office. I'm sure it was just a coincidence, but having such a symbol of success on me at the moment I crossed her path probably opened a door.

———◆———

When speaking the language of Success, make sure you know all the local customs of adornment. You'll get a lot farther with the natives that way.

When you think about grooming, accessorizing, putting on makeup, shaving, ironing your clothes, or whatever else makes you look like the top performers in your industry, if your first thought is, "I couldn't be bothered," just remember that the successful people do bother. They bother every day, which is part of the reason they're where they are. Dress for success.

CHAPTER THIRTEEN

KEY PHRASES IN THE LANGUAGE OF SUCCESS

Some of the first things you learn in any new language are a few common phrases to help you navigate the territory if you find yourself lost and in need of directions.

There are thousands of phrases that could come in handy while learning to speak Success. The list below is only a partial sampling, carefully curated to reflect the values in this book. They are for the self-starter, the dreamer, the fighter, and the person who wasn't born on third base – or even in the ball park.

If you are struggling to be fluent in Success, memorize a few of these phrases to ease your interactions with the locals. Find the ones that apply to you and live by them.

What is not included here are quotes along the lines of, "There's plenty of time to sleep when you're dead," or, "Have a singular goal and exclude all other pursuits until you reach it." I firmly believe that success should not come at the sacrifice of your health, your relationships or your happiness. If you define success as an abundance of money or power without any other rewards, that's fine, but then you may want to augment this list of quotes with some that better suit your needs.

If, however, your definition of success reflects a humane approach to reaching your goals while maintaining balance with all other endeavors, these key phrases will be of great use to you.

Also not included in this list are quotes along the lines of Walt Disney's statement that, "All your dreams come true if you just work hard enough." Let's all agree that that's simply not true. There are literally millions of incredibly hard working people in the world whose dreams are not coming true. I work in Hollywood. I see some people putting in 12-15 hour days to pursue a dream of success in the entertainment business and others who were lucky enough to sit next to the right person on an airplane.

There are many, many factors in anyone achieving success, including an element of good luck, and to suggest that someone who hasn't reached their peak isn't working hard enough is just cruel. Yes, there are those who could work harder and get farther, but I want you, the reader of this book, to be inspired, not insulted or discouraged.

The quotes below are reminders, maxims and mottos that can really help you out of a rut, or give you a boost to keep going when things get tough. They can help you halt a failure spiral or inspire you to make that next phone call or write that next email.

Pick your favorites and memorize them. Share them with others. Put them on post-it notes at your desk or inside your wallet, just as little reminders of your new language, until you are fluent.

Not all of them will resonate with you. Feel free to ignore those that will not help you learn your new language, and add any that may not be included here. This collection is not definitive – it's just a starter set.

Enjoy!

"Start where you are. Use what you have. Do what you can."
— Arthur Ashe

"Though no one can go back and make a brand-new start, anyone can start from now and make a brand-new ending."
— Carl Bard

"Be patient with yourself. Self-growth is tender; it's holy ground. There's no greater investment."
— Stephen Covey

"It does not matter how slowly you go, so long as you do not stop."

– Confucius

"Someone is sitting in the shade today because someone planted a tree a long time ago."

– Warren Buffett

"Live as if you were to die tomorrow. Learn as if you were to live forever."

– Mahatma Gandhi

"The difference between winning and losing is most often not quitting."

– Walt Disney

"You must expect great things of yourself before you can do them."

– Michael Jordan

"Don't limit yourself. Many people limit themselves to what they think they can do. You can only go as far as your mind lets you."

– Mary Kay Ash

"If you are going through hell, keep going."
— Winston Churchill

"A dream doesn't become reality through magic; it takes sweat, determination and hard work."
— Colin Powell

"The biggest risk is not taking any risk… In a world that's changing really quickly, the only strategy that is guaranteed to fail is not taking risks."
— Mark Zuckerberg

"Don't be afraid to give up the good to go for the great."
— John D. Rockefeller

"It is never too late to be what you might have been."
— George Eliot

"I have not failed. I've just found 10,000 ways that won't work."
— Thomas A. Edison

"In the middle of every difficulty lies opportunity."
— Albert Einstein

"Your time is limited, so don't waste it living someone else's life."

— Steve Jobs

"There are no mistakes, only opportunities."

— Tina Fey

"The best way of learning about anything is by doing."

— Richard Branson

"Efforts and courage are not enough without purpose and direction."

— John F. Kennedy

"Don't let the fear of striking out hold you back."

— Babe Ruth

"Always remember, you have within you the strength, the patience and the passion to reach for the stars to change the world."

— Harriet Tubman

"If there is no struggle, there is no progress."

— Frederick Douglass

"It is our choices that show what we truly are, far more than our abilities."

– J. K Rowling

"Whether you think you can or you think you can't, you're right."

– Henry Ford

"If you don't build your dream, someone else will hire you to help them build theirs."

– Dhirubhai Ambani

"The first step toward success is taken when you refuse to be a captive of the environment in which you first find yourself."

– Mark Caine

"People who succeed have momentum. The more they succeed, the more they want to succeed, and the more they find a way to succeed. Similarly, when someone is failing, the tendency is to get on a downward spiral that can even become a self-fulfilling prophecy."

– Tony Robbins

"When I dare to be powerful — to use my strength in the service of my vision, then it becomes less and less important whether I am afraid."

— Audre Lorde

"People who are crazy enough to think they can change the world, are the ones who do."

Steve Jobs

"A successful man is one who can lay a firm foundation with the bricks others have thrown at him."

— David Brinkley

"The successful warrior is the average man, with laser-like focus."

— Bruce Lee

Develop success from failures. Discouragement and failure are two of the surest stepping stones to success."

— Dale Carnegie

"If you don't design your own life plan, chances are you'll fall into someone else's plan. And guess what they have planned for you? Not much."

– Jim Rohn

"If you genuinely want something, don't wait for it – teach yourself to be impatient."

– Gurbaksh Chahal

"If you want to make a permanent change, stop focusing on the size of your problems and start focusing on the size of you!"

– T. Harv Eker

"If you are not willing to risk the usual you will have to settle for the ordinary."

– Jim Rohn

"Success is walking from failure to failure with no loss of enthusiasm."

– Winston Churchill

"What seems to us as bitter trials are often blessings in disguise."

– Oscar Wilde

"There are two types of people who will tell you that you cannot make a difference in this world: those who are afraid to try and those who are afraid you will succeed."

– Ray Goforth

"The starting point of all achievement is desire."

– Napolean Hill

"Success is the sum of small efforts, repeated day-in and day-out."

– Robert Collier

"If you want to achieve excellence, you can get there today. As of this second, quit doing less-than-excellent work."

– Thomas J. Watson

"Courage is resistance to fear, mastery of fear - not absence of fear."

– Mark Twain

"People often say that motivation doesn't last. Well, neither does bathing - that's why we do it daily."

– Zig Ziglar

"The only place where success comes before work is in the dictionary."

–Vidal Sassoon

"The reason most people never reach their goals is that they don't define them, or ever seriously consider them as believable or achievable."

– Denis Watiley

"Motivation is what gets you started. Habit is what keeps you going."

– Jim Ryun

"There is no chance, no destiny, no fate, that can hinder or control the firm resolve of a determined soul."

– Ella Wheeler Wilcox

"You've got to get up every morning with determination if you're going to go to bed with satisfaction."

– George Lorimer

"To be successful you must accept all challenges that come your way. You can't just accept the ones you like."

– Mike Gafka

"To accomplish great things, we must not only act, but also dream, not only plan, but also believe."

– Anatole France

"You measure the size of the accomplishment by the obstacles you had to overcome to reach your goals."

– Booker T. Washington

"Real difficulties can be overcome; it is only the imaginary ones that are unconquerable."

– Theodore N. Vail

"Fortune sides with him who dares."

– Virgil

"Failure is the condiment that gives success its flavor."

– Truman Capote

"Don't let what you cannot do interfere with what you can do."

– John R. Wooden

"A person can be as great as he or she wants to be. If you believe in yourself and have the courage, the determination, the dedication, the competitive drive and if you are willing to sacrifice the little things in life and pay the price for the things that are worthwhile, it can be done."

–Vince Lombardi

"Things work out best for those who make the best of how things work out."

– John Wooden

"Entrepreneurs average 3.8 failures before final success. What sets the successful ones apart is their amazing persistence."

– Lisa M. Amos

"It is not the strongest of the species that survive, nor the most intelligent, but the one most responsive to change."

– Charles Darwin

FINAL THOUGHTS ABOUT SUCCESS

I was giving a talk to a group of attorneys recently and I mentioned this book, and that it is for anyone who might not have been raised learning the skills needed for success. One woman said, "Be sure to tell them not to do anything that the lawyers on TV do."

Of course, she was absolutely right about people on television and in movies. I have yet to see a lawyer or an investment banker created by a screenwriter who even comes close to behaving the way one is supposed to in the real world, and even worse are the cast members on so-called "Reality" shows, where the more conflict you create, the longer the producers want to keep you around.

Their primary job – the television lawyers, bankers, chefs, fashion designers, doctors, nurses, teachers and others – is to be entertaining, not to represent the client, save the patient or make the best dress. Please do not use them as examples of how to behave in those professions, because most of their behavior will get you fired on the first day.

But all of that got me thinking a lot about role models and mentors and how people find them, and who makes a good one or a bad one. The truth is, we all have much better role models in our lives than we may realize, and although things in this book may be new to you, or different from what you've been taught in the past, I'd bet a lot more of it is stuff you already learned somewhere along the way, just not in the direct way presented here.

For example, your parents may not have been corporate titans, but did you ever overhear one of them on the phone, negotiating to get a late charge removed from a credit card bill or to keep the power from being shut off? If so, you got a very good lesson in which negotiating tactics work and which don't. You learned that it is always best to ask for what you need, and you may have made some notes to yourself about planning and saving and prioritizing that are serving you well today.

The truth is, the home you grew up in did prepare you for success. I know this because you are still alive and reading this book, which means you have survival instincts and a desire to reach beyond your current situation, so thank whoever raised you for both of those things.

There are seven billion people on this planet and each one was born into a situation that could enhance or hinder their chances of defining and achieving personal success. A tribesman who has four wives and six goats may be the epitome of success in his community, or he may desire to move to a place where he can study to become an architecht. Even if he was groomed since birth to run the tribe and own the goats, he still has to learn skills that will take him where he wants to be, regardless of the advantages he was born with.

As long as you continue to strive and grow beyond your original station in life, you will continue to feel less than instinctively prepared for the challenges of your journey, and guess what? Everyone working to develop the skills needed to succeed on their own terms feels the same way. That is perfectly normal and you are in great company.

You have all the tools within you to be a success. Practice honing and using them properly and soon you will be able to marvel at what you have built.

ABOUT THE AUTHOR

Valerie Alexander is an author, speaker, filmmaker and coach. Valerie's books include *Happiness as a Second Language* an Amazon #1 Seller in the Happiness and Self-Help categories, *Success as a Second Language* and *How Women Can Succeed in the Workplace (Despite Having "Female Brains")*, based on her popular talk.

As a screenwriter, her projects have included the adaptation of the novel *Social Crimes* for Phoenix Pictures, with Joel Schumacher attached to direct, the adaptation of Michael Chepiga's stage play, *Getting & Spending*, for Catherine Zeta Jones, the development of the television series *Gangster, Inc.* for CubeVision, and numerous original screenplays in various stages of development.

Valerie made her directing debut with the award-winning short film *Making the Cut*, and she is the creator, producer and director of "Say I Do," "Life Support," and "The Wedding Matters," highly successful commercial campaigns in support of marriage equality.

Prior to becoming a screenwriter, Valerie was a corporate securities lawyer, a venture capital consultant, an investment banker, and the V.P. of Business Development for PixelWorld Networks.

Before entering the professional ranks, Valerie worked as a horse wrangler, an algebra teacher, a runway model, a tutor for the developmentally disabled, an amusement park supervisor, an SAT, GRE & LSAT prep teacher, and the world's worst waitress.

Valerie received her B.A. from Trinity University and her J.D. and M.S. degrees from the University of California, Berkeley. In the spring of 2010, she returned to Berkeley Law to teach the legal ethics seminar, *Representation of Law in Film.*

Valerie and her husband, writer-producer, Rick Alexander, live in Los Angeles, CA, with their ill-mannered German Shepherd, Pepper.

To join Valerie's Happiness mailing list and get two free Happiness Workbooks, please go to **http://www.speakhappiness.com/hello/**.

To join her Success mailing list, please go to www.speakhappiness.com/SSL.

OTHER BOOKS BY VALERIE ALEXANDER

Happiness as a Second Language: A Guidebook for Achieving Lasting, Permanent Happiness

How Women Can Succeed in the Workplace (Despite Having "Female Brains")

Thank you for reading this book in the "...as a Second Language" series. May Happiness and Success be yours, today and always.

—Valerie Alexander

22118450R00125

Made in the USA
San Bernardino, CA
20 June 2015